To My Loving Daughter
Denise Michelle Krivitsky
Always There When I Need Her

1

Other Books in this series of
TRUE ADVENTURE STORIES FROM THE CIVIL WAR:

- **Corydon — The Forgotten Battle Of The Civil War**
  By W. Fred Conway
- **The Most Incredible Prison Escape Of The Civil War**
  By W. Fred Conway
- **Quantrill — The Wildest Killer Of The Civil War And Other Stories**
  By Paul Ditzel

If not available at your favorite bookstore, you may order direct from the publisher at $9.95 each plus $3.00 shipping and handling.

FBH Publishers
P.O. Box 711, New Albany, IN 47151
Phone 1-800-457-2400

Library of Congress Cataloging in Publication Data
Ditzel, Paul

The Ruthless Exploits Of Admiral John Winslow —
Naval Hero Of The Civil War
Library of Congress Catalog Number: 91-070889
ISBN 0-925165-05-0

FBH Publishers, P.O. Box 711, New Albany, IN 47151-0711
© Paul Ditzel 1991

Typography and Layout: Pam Jones
Cover: Ron Grunder

THE RUTHLESS EXPLOITS OF

ADMIRAL JOHN WINSLOW —

Naval Hero of The Civil War

Paul Ditzel

CONTENTS

John Ancrum Winslow, as a lad in coastal Wilmington, North Carolina, often watched the ships in Wilmington's harbor, and fantasized about the adventures of his great grandfather.

In the early 1700's, William Rhett had led the colonists to a sea victory over a Franco-Spanish expedition that attacked Charleston, South Carolina. Rhett's volunteer navy killed, wounded, or captured 300 of the invaders.

Next, great grandfather Rhett chased Bluebeard The Pirate and caught him off Cape Fear. He took Bluebeard and his crew prisoner. These swashbuckling adventures caught young Winslow's fancy, and he found himself reenacting them while he spent long hours watching the ships in the harbor.

Little did he dream that one day he would win even greater acclaim as the man who sent to the bottom another buccaneer, whose depredations made Bluebeard's appear trifling by comparison.

Chapter One

Baptism By
Mexican Fire

Navy Lieutenant John Winslow crouched in the bow of his barge on that humid afternoon of October 29, 1846. Turning to his men he wondered whether his own face was as streaked with the sweat and grime of the dank Mexican jungle as theirs.

"Keep low!" whispered Winslow. "They're liable to start shooting any minute." The knot in the throat of the chunky young officer with the squarish-face and dark hair made it hard for him to talk, and he hoped his tone did not betray his tension at this, his first real baptism of fire.

Winslow peered over the barge's railing and studied the silent adobe fort guarding the town of Tabasco, 72 miles upstream from the gulf. The tropic chaparral overhanging the river offered excellent cover for snipers. He felt hundreds of eyes in the fort and the jungle watching his barge and the dozen others bobbing impatiently on the slime-covered water.

"What's Perry waiting for?" muttered Winslow. Almost an hour ago the commodore had sent a message to Mexican General Bravo demanding that he surrender the fort. So far, no answer. "Night will soon fall and we'll have to withdraw or worry about boarding, unless we strike now and establish a beachhead." Winslow nervously pinched the fuzzy beginnings of chin whiskers that were the vogue among seamen aboard the blockading fleet in the Gulf of Mexico.

"I suppose we'll find that this Perry is *another* politician!" snorted Winslow. "Just like that fool Conner. They always hanky-panky back and forth all day until it's too late to fight." It had been this way since the war started and Commodore David Conner's procrastination finally resulted in Commodore Matthew Perry being sent down to beef up the Navy's participation. The Tabasco assault was Perry's first since he arrived.

The commandant at Tabasco, General Bravo, had been taunting Conner for failing to attack. Bravo hid behind the geographical fact that a sandbar at the mouth of the river afforded him ample reason for his derision especially when the schooner *USS McLane* grounded at Alvarado near the river's entrance. Bravo never reckoned upon the aggressiveness of Perry, who wanted to capture the Mexican fleet of shallow draft boats at Tabasco. The commodore had outfitted a fleet of special barges for this bold attack deep into the Mexican interior.

"If it's a fight Bravo's begging for, why don't we make him put his guns where his mouth is," wondered Winslow, swatting the mosquito that landed on his wrist. He conceded that Perry probably proposed to do just that but he would have preferred to omit the diplomatic niceties preceding attack.

"Surrender, sir!" Perry signaled again. Winslow fidgeted.

"Go to hell, sir," said Bravo. "Fire as soon as you please!"

We'll do that!" snapped Winslow who felt the concussions as Perry's temporary flagship, the steam gunboat

Commodore Matthew Perry was sent down to beef up the U.S. Navy's participation in the Mexican War. He outranked Winslow, then a young Lieutenant, who resented Perry's taking over. Winslow disobeyed Perry's orders, refused to surrender, and ordered his men to attack.

Vixen, lobbed three quick shells into the fort. One shot cut down the flagpole, and the Mexican ensign fell. The other two panicked the garrison, and the troops fled Tabasco, leaving only a hard core of swarthy guerrillas whose muskets opened up on the barges.

"Proceed with landing operations," ordered Perry. The beachhead was quickly taken although the guerillas immediately pinned the Marines down with a peppery hail of musket balls. As Winslow's barge headed for the beach, he noticed that Lieutenant Condee's boat was drifting dangerously close to a pocket of snipers who were shifting their fire from the main landing onto Condee.

"There they are!" pointed Winslow. "Up on the roofs of those mud flats. We'll take 'em ourselves!" His men bent to the oars, and Winslow leaped overboard before the barge scraped the muddy shore.

Winslow and his men were better marksmen than the snipers, and he whooped as the last of them pitched headfirst from the roof. Winslow hesitated. His orders were to make the landing, hold the beach, and wait for Perry's order to advance. But Winslow was cut off from the main body and what the commodore didn't know would not hurt him. Certainly Perry could not object if he struck out on his own.

"Come on!" Winslow shouted, urging his men forward. "Make the most of this!" They knew what Perry's orders were, but if the young lieutenant wanted to take it upon himself to overrule the commodore, it wasn't their stripes which would be forfeited.

Winslow's squad hugged the sides of the pueblos as they advanced several hundred yards up the dusty street. He spotted another group of snipers hiding in a mud building. Musket balls sizzled past his ear. That's as close as the shots ever came. Winslow's squad quickly wiped out those guerrillas, too.

"Let's go, boys!" Winslow yelled, as the older men rallied to the enthusiasm of their boyish leader. Another block further and they were crouching at the edge of the town square. A volley sent Winslow and his men diving for cover behind a mule cart.

"Judging from all that firing, there must be a big gang of 'em holed up over there," Winslow said, nodding toward a barracks-like building diagonally across the plaza.

"You keep 'em busy," Winslow told his men. "I'll go back and get the order to attack. We'll storm the barracks and take the town before old Bravo knows what hit him!"

Winslow ran back to the beach where Marine Captain Edson's men were returning sporadic fire from the house tops while awaiting orders to move into Tabasco.

"What the hell are you doing way up there?" asked Edson.

"I've got a gang of 'em cornered in a barracks. Just say the word and I'll drive the bastards out."

"No. Winslow. You can't advance."

"Can't advance! In God's name why?"

"Our orders are to hold the beach until Perry says to attack."

"But I..."

"Lieutenant!" interrupted Edson. "I told you to stand fast!"

In the light of future events it's just as well that Captain Edson did not overhear Winslow's mutterings as he returned dejectedly to his men.

Commodore Perry heard the sharp firing and saw a cloud of gunsmoke rising from the center of Tabasco.

"Sounds like a real hassle is going on back in there," Perry commented. "Wonder who got signals crossed and drove that far into town? If I'd known we could take Tabasco this easily I'd have given the order for attack. It's too late to do more today." Perry signaled the skirmishers to return to their barges.

"Return!" snapped Winslow when the runner brought the order. "Why?"

"Because it's getting dark," replied the messenger, testily. "Perry says so."

Choking down his disgust, Winslow and his men fell back to the shore. He was keenly disappointed that this engagement should end so indecisively. Winslow had not lost a man, but he sorely hated to give up what he had won. It wasn't Navy-like to quit.

At dawn the townspeople waved white flags from their rooftops, but most of the guerrillas ignored Tabasco's offer to surrender. Perry decided the town was not important enough to occupy and gave the order to gather together the prize boats they had captured without resistance and return to the blockading fleet. As a parting souvenir Perry silenced the guerrillas by ordering his gunboats to lay a murderous fire into the chaparral and along the main streets.

Winslow was still rankled as the strong current quickly carried the flotilla down river. He had to admit the mission was successful. They had bagged nine vessels: two steamers, a brig, a sloop, and five schooners. Winslow knew their value lay not so much in their potential striking power, for they were pathetically frail craft. Rather, their light draft would make them handy for future expeditions over sandbars and up the hundreds of small streams penetrating far into Mexico.

Equally important, the Tabasco expedition boosted

the sagging morale of the blockaders. The most action they had seen since the war started was fighting off mosquitoes, yellow fever, scurvy, ague, and savage storms that pounded the ships in winter.

When Perry reached his anchorage at Anton Lizardo near Vera Cruz, he reconstructed the events at Tabasco and learned that Winslow was the courageous young officer who had conveniently disregarded orders while brazenly jabbing deep into the town despite heavy musket fire. Who *was* this youth, Perry wondered. If he was a heller on land what might he be in command of a ship?

Winslow could indeed be a heller, but just how much of one Perry had no way of knowing, which is perhaps fortunate for this brash lieutenant who was destined to become the "Bad Boy" of the Civil War's Union Navy.

Chapter Two

He Called Lincoln
A Chowderhead

Winslow could always be counted upon to do the unexpected. The call of the sea was all-consuming to him, but an auburn-haired beauty would drive him close to forsaking it. Winslow was a native southerner who would stand by the North, although he considered President Lincoln a "chowderhead" and did not hesitate to say so publicly. As a rebellious Yankee, he would be accused of insubordination and of treason in leaking naval weaknesses to the Confederacy. Yet, when the South lay in defeat, Winslow leaped at the chance to clobber helpless New Orleans insensible with his fleet of ironclads.

Winslow made it plain he thought most of his superior officers were idiots. He accused them of being responsible for the loss of a revolutionary new type of frigate because they were too hard-headed to listen to an enlisted man's advice; that their laxity also cost him his own first command and that a young sailor was murdered to save the reputation of a dilly-dallying commodore.

Winslow would become so irritated at the tradition-bound Navy brass for turning down an invention that might have shortened the Civil War that he vowed he would sell the idea to Russia. All this is not to suggest, however, that there was not a good-sized kernel of truth in what he popped off about.

Winslow's outspokenness and amazing penchant for antagonizing Washington would continually keep him in hot water. He held politicians and diplomats in equal contempt, and his peculiar art of plain talk would someday provoke an international incident between the United States and England, and threaten our relations with France.

Had it not been for Winslow's outspokenness, however, the Union might never have tasted the sweet coup of victory when the hated Raphael Semmes, Winslow's former friend and messmate, whose career ironically paralleled his own, was whipped in the most spectacular high seas battle of the war. Except for a blooper which shadowed Winslow's triumph, he might have ranked in immortality with Admiral David Farragut, who said he would have gladly missed the capture of New Orleans if only he could have duplicated Winslow's brilliant naval feat.

John Ancrum Winslow was born November 19, 1811, in Wilmington, North Carolina. He was the second of Sara and Edward Winslow's four children. Among his ancestors was a Mayflower Pilgrim. The elder Winslow hoped his son would follow him in commercial work, but as a boy he was intrigued by his mother's stories of Great Grandfather William Rhett, who distinguished himself by leading an improvised fleet of six small ships against a Franco-Spanish expedition that attacked Charleston in 1704. Rhett whipped the invaders, killing, wounding and capturing 300 of them.

Eleven years later Rhett chased Bluebeard the Pirate and caught up with him off Cape Fear. He took Bluebeard prisoner along with his crew and brig. These swashbuckling adventures caught young Winslow's fancy, and he found himself reenacting them while he spent hours watching the

16

ships in Wilmington harbor. Winslow never dreamed that some day he would win greater acclaim as the man who sent to the bottom another buccaneer whose depredations made Bluebeard's appear trifling by comparison.

Young John was too shy to invite himself aboard any of the men-o'-war tied up at the docks until the afternoon he stood gazing out to sea with his brother, Edward. John heard a movement behind him. Turning, he took the full force of a hard right from a lanky cabin boy off a nearby English frigate. Its crew had promised the bully a prize if he would deck the two youths standing near the end of the wharf.

Winslow's tongue tasted the blood flowing from his split lip. The bully seemed eager for more fight. John shoved his brother out of the way. He stepped up to the cabin boy and landed an uppercut that he could only have learned from long experience along the docks. The jolting wallop lifted the bully two inches off the wharf. He landed in a heap near a capstan. The British tars cheered Winslow and hurried down the gangplank to raise his arm in victory. He refused the prize they offered him and instead asked to see the ship.

The sailors lifted Winslow to their shoulders and carried him aboard the frigate, where they treated him to an odd-tasting liquid that looked like weak tea but had a bitter, syrupy taste. Winslow, his eyes and innards aglow from rum, went home that night determined he would follow the call of the sea.

Years passed before Winslow would get his parents' permission to join the Navy. Patience was not among his stronger traits, however, and John talked Edward into setting out to see the world. They stole a rowboat and erected a bush for a sail. The wind and tide quickly swept them out to sea and the two nonchalantly settled back to enjoy their first ocean cruise. The salt air soon put them to sleep.

The Winslow Estate at Marshfield, Massachusetts, which Daniel Webster leased from John Winslow's father.

Daniel Webster mixed farming and politics while at the Winslow estate. He used his influence to get young John Winslow an appointment to Midshipman's School.

18

Had it not been for the lookout in the crow's nest of an inbound schooner, the voyage would have been Winslow's first and last. The ship picked up the boys and brought them into Wilmington, where hundreds had turned out to look for them and drag the waters around John's favorite dock. Mrs. Winslow was convinced her boys had been shanghaied.

Winslow's father, realizing John was not suited for the humdrum life of a businessman, took his problem to Daniel Webster, who lived on the Winslow estate at Marshfield. Webster listened sympathetically and then obtained a naval appointment for John. In midshipmen's school the boy avidly absorbed everything nautical. He had time for little else but his studies. Not even the eager young girls at nearby schools seemed able to lure him from his navigation books.

Winslow's first assignment was aboard the *USS Falmouth*. For him it was a dream cruise. The *Falmouth* was ordered to the West Indies, and for three years Winslow relived the adventures of his great grandfather while taking part in small boat expeditions against island haunts of pirates.

Winslow returned home when he was 21, completed his examinations, and was promoted to Passed Midshipman. The Navy put him on standby duty at the Boston Navy Yard while awaiting orders. His messmates were somewhat puzzled when they noticed "The Grind", as they called him because of his prepossession with things maritime, was spending more and more of his spare time ashore.

Three months later when Winslow reported for duty aboard the *USS Erie* bound for the Brazilian Squadron, his shipmates were dumbfounded when they looked over the rail and saw "The Grind" walking slowly down the quay arm-in-arm with a shapely auburn-haired beauty of obvious refinement, judging from the modest way she tried but could not possibly conceal definite contours of interest under her fluffy pink and white calico dress. Their lingering kiss was nothing short of scandalous in staid Beantown and provided Winslow's shipmates with something to discuss in detail during their entire first week at sea. He was evasive about her name but slipped once and referred to her as "My Kathy."

Four years later when Winslow returned to Boston he married Kathy—Catherine Amelia Winslow, his first cousin. The wedding raised many eyebrows in Puritan Boston and caused a good deal of comment in his own family. The couple settled in suburban Roxbury while Winslow awaited new orders. Before long other scandals diverted the city's wagging tongues.

Winslow was positive his honeymoon would be short, and he made the most of it preparatory to shipping out. However, for a married man whose first love supposedly was the sea, Winslow showed a peculiar amount of unbounded joy when he was assigned to shore duty in the Boston Navy Yard.

Kathy was all and more that Winslow could expect in a wife. In time she was to win a battle over her competitor, and Kathy took the place of the men as Winslow's first love. It would take quite a woman to do that, which was exactly what Kathy was. She bore him seven children, five sons and two daughters.

Two years and one child after their wedding, Winslow was promoted to Lieutenant and again ordered to Brazil aboard the U.S. schooner *Enterprise*, but in his weakened condition from the rigors of shore duty he fell ill from an attack of tropic fevers and was returned to Boston where he recovered with amazing speed.

In July, 1842, while war clouds were forming over Mexico, Winslow was chosen for one of the most envious assignments in the Navy: duty aboard the spanking new

USS Missouri, a revolutionary steam paddle frigate that a young Captain by the name of Matthew Calbraith Perry was championing as the fighting ship of the future.

The *Missouri* and her hand-picked crew cruised up and down the Atlantic Coast to show the public the Navy's new plaything. Then she set sail for the Mediterranean on a goodwill trip and also to carry Caleb Cushing, the new Minister to China, as far as Alexandria, Egypt.

Winslow stood proudly at attention in his newly-pressed uniform as the *Missouri*, the first armed naval steamship to cross the Atlantic, came into Gibraltar. Spyglasses were trained upon the razor sharp frigate as her paddle wheels smartly slapped the water. British Navy officers hurried aboard to salute the new ship and examine her closely.

Winslow pointed out to the visitors that she was a perfect specimen of naval architecture. She weighed 2200 tons, had four copper boilers, two inclined engines which could deliver 600 horsepower, and was bark-rigged for sailing. Winslow was especially proud of her firepower, a pair of 240-pound guns, the largest afloat. For extra measure she carried ten 68-pounders.

The *Missouri* spent two days in Gibraltar, and the night before she sailed Winslow went ashore with the other officers for a farewell party in their honor. Aboard ship two crewmen were lagging a cylinder by lamp light. A third sailor went into the storeroom above them to get a pair of scales and accidentally dropped a wrench onto a demijohn of turpentine. The liquid from the broken bottle spilled down upon the cylinder, soaked the lagging, and was ignited by the lamp.

The revelry at the champagne and caviar party was so boisterous that Winslow and the others almost failed to hear the screaming outside. "El Frigate vapor Americano es del Fuego!"

Chapter Three

The Inexcusable Execution

"Quiet!" said Winslow. "What's that yelling about?"

The American steamer is on fire!"

Winslow and the others ran half a mile to the docks and stopped short when they reached the water wall.

"Good Lord!" breathed Winslow. A fountain of flame was spouting as high as the *Missouri's* maintop. He jumped aboard Captain John Newton's gig and was rowed to the ship. The fire cast a shimmering glow across the waters. Winslow could feel the heat when he was still 100 yards away.

As he approached the *Missouri*, Winslow heard her fire pumps throbbing. "If the flames ever reach the forward magazine we're done for," he muttered, scampering up the ladder.

The wind drove clouds of smoke into Winslow's face. He took charge of one of the firefighting gangs and led them down a smoky companionway. The pungent stink of the burning oils, turpentine and oakum made him retch.

"Harder there on those pumps," he yelled to the crew-men at a water tank. The sailors speeded up the tempo of their strokes, but the stream was pitifully ineffective against

23

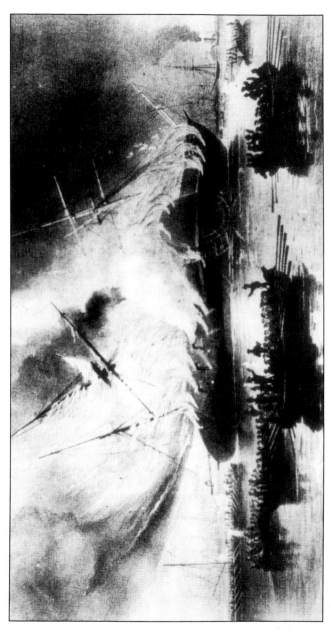

The USS Missouri, a revolutionary new steam paddle frigate, with a hand-picked crew including Lieutenant John Winslow, burned and sank when an oil lamp ignited spilled turpentine. Winslow's desperate attempt to save her was in vain.

the boiling cauldron of flames. The terrific heat and suffocating smoke mauled Winslow backwards, and the water turned to steam before it bored into the heart of the fire. The *Missouri* was doomed.

"Every man save himself!" bawled Captain Newton.

"Please sir," pleaded Winslow. "Just let me try a bit longer."

"It's no use, lieutenant, we can never save her. Get off now while there's still time. The magazine is sure to blow any minute."

Winslow ran to his cabin to save some of his belongings, and got lost in the dense smoke. Turning to flee down the companionway, he found he was cut off by two wings of the fire that had melded. Heat singed his hair, and his uniform smoldered. His lungs strained to the bursting point, and he felt himself losing consciousness.

Winslow's fingers finally found a porthole on the gun deck. He squeezed through it and dropped into the water. As he reached a longboat, Winslow gulped fresh air and saw he was one of the last to leave the ship. The rowers put their shoulders to the oars in a desperate race to reach safety before the raging fire touched off the magazine.

Winslow looked back toward the *Missouri*. Flames shrouded the badly listing frigate, illuminated the entire harbor, and cast a weird glow on the rock of Gibraltar. Jets of fire spewed from her gunports, and streaks of flame raced up her rigging, spread out along her yardarms, and gnawed furiously into the canvas.

The intense heat touched off a 68-pound gun's saluting cartridge. Flaming debris and firebrands rocketed high into the sky. Before Winslow could catch his breath, the concussion set off the forward magazine. The blast knocked him flat in the boat, and he got to his knees as the frigate's towering masts toppled into the water. The flaming hulk of the pride of the American Navy was soon swallowed by the sea and the daylight glow in Gibraltar turned pitch black again.

Captain Newton sent Winslow back to the United States with dispatches describing the affair. Winslow was bitter at the loss of the *Missouri*. Had the thick-skulled Navy brass listened to Engineer Haswell, inflammable liquids would have been stored in metal cans. But the officers had rejected the idea the *Missouri* could burn.

Winslow landed in Boston after midnight and immediately went to Roxbury. His home was dark. He crept under Kathy's window and softly sang a love song of the day:

> "Gaily the troubador touched his guitar
> As he was hastening home from the war,
> Singing, 'From Palestine hither I come,
> Lady-love, lady-love, welcome me home.'"

Winslow gasped when he saw the window fly open. There stood Kathy in a filmy robin's egg blue nightgown that was never intended to conceal her charms, nor designed for its wearer to stand in open windows on a cold night.

"Why, John, is that you?"

"Yes, darling!"

"What are you *ever* doing home?"

"Come down, let me in and I'll tell you."

Some time later the dispatches arrived in Washington, and Winslow returned to Gibraltar. While awaiting a new ship, he accepted the Marquis de Lorne's invitation to a boar hunt in Tangiers. Winslow was game to try anything new, and found himself in the exacting company of British Army and Navy officers, all of them experienced horsemen. "I can ride anything you've got," he boasted.

His horse had galloped only a hundred yards when Winslow realized he should not have been so outspoken about his equestrian ability. This was the first and last time in his life he ever regretted speaking out. A hurricane at sea was preferable to his jouncing.

Winslow fell far behind the pack, lost his way, and unceremoniously galloped into a bed of quicksand. The others, noticing their American friend was missing, started to look for him, and when they found Winslow he had sunk to his waist. They hauled him out, and he quietly walked his mount back to the stable, vowing he would never again get on a horse.

Winslow returned to the United States and was assigned to the *USS Cumberland*, Conner's flagship, for Mexican war duty. General Zachary Taylor's troops were slicing through the enemy as if their battlements were sand. There remained little for the Gulf Squadron to do but blockade the coast, a pointless tactic on the Navy Department's part, Winslow felt. Mexico had no merchant marine and fewer friends willing to try to run in supplies on the country's shaky credit. Her navy was almost imaginary, and what few ships she had never ventured out under Conner's guns.

Life aboard the *Cumberland* was like a prison. Why didn't the commodore do *something* to give the Navy a chance to shine along with the Army? Even the most insignificant assault against the coast or a daring thrust up one of Mexico's rivers would make the Navy look good at home. The American press was thirsting for feats like the glorious ones of the War of 1812 and was editorially disappointed when the commodore reported no spectacular sea fights or invasions.

"Conner is too damned afraid of getting his hands dirty in the swamplands," grumbled Winslow who recalled the commodore's reputation as "The Best Dressed Officer in the Navy."

In July Winslow and his men captured a small Mexican boat that seemed ideally suited for carrying fresh water from shore to the fleet. Winslow was all for pitching its haughty Mexican captain overboard and letting him swim to shore.

Conner, however, accepted the Mexican's offer of help if his boat was returned. He invited the commodore to be his guest at his hacienda, and promised the squadron would be treated to ample water, fresh fruits and provisions. The fleet sailed at dawn and headed for the beach designated by the Mexican. Small boats from each ship headed in to get water.

Winslow was uneasy. He felt he was being watched. But the Mexican seemed amiable enough. "Perhaps I'm wrong," thought Winslow.

As the second group of boats headed in, a scouting party of Marines reached the summit of a brush-covered hill overlooking the watering spot and stumbled onto a large band of guerrillas getting into position to ambush the boats. The Marines sounded the alarm, opened fire on the Mexicans, and ran back to the beach to the boats. The guerrillas returned the shots and wounded one crewman.

Safe at last aboard the *Cumberland*, Winslow snorted his disgust at Conner's gullibility, and shuddered at his own narrow escape. "Fresh provisions for the commodore! What a blockhead he is!"

Driven to action by newspaper criticism, Conner at last decided to make an assault against the town of Alvarado, and sent a squadron of mosquito boats up the Tabasco River. Winslow eagerly prepared for battle. This was an operation almost certain of success, and Winslow's enthusiasm mounted as the squadron sailed for Alvarado. Two British men-o'-war made a holiday of the assault and accompanied the Americans to watch them make sport of the dinky Mexican boats and inept fort guarding the town.

Conner lined his ships in an impressive battle formation outside Alvarado, and Winslow finished his preparations to lead a landing force. Conner's lookout reported from the crow's nest that a group of 200, no, closer to 1,000 Mexican soldiers were heading for the beach. The lookout's first estimate was closer to the truth, but Conner lost his nerve and signaled the flotilla to withdraw after firing a dozen shells into the antiquated fort.

Winslow swore with frustration as the squadron steamed away. "That old maid! Frightened off by a pack of peasants and a mud fort with five museum pieces for guns!" His face flushed with embarrassment when he imagined the derision rocking the British ships as they watched the Americans run from a band of poorly armed and worse trained Mexicans.

Matters raced to a climax early in September. The crew of the sloop *USS St. Mary's* sent Conner a letter complaining about the way their officers were treating them. The commodore started a secret investigation, and when the *St. Mary's* officers learned of it they took their bitterness out on the crew. A sailor retaliated by punching a *St. Mary's* lieutenant in the jaw, knocking him unconscious on the deck.

The sailor was found guilty by a court martial and sentenced to death. The trial board privately admitted they expected Conner to recommend leniency, but overlooked the commodore's fear of what Washington might say. If he commuted the sailor's sentence, Washington would feel Conner had lost control of discipline in his fleet.

Winslow stood helplessly at attention as the officers and men were piped to witness punishment. "It's murder! That's what it is," he muttered. Winslow winced when the screaming young sailor, barely out of his teens, was half-carried and dragged up on deck from the brig and made to climb the main mast to the yard arm. Winslow's heart beat faster and faster as the death sentence was read. The youth shrieked for mercy. Beads of sweat ran down Winslow's back. The oil-slicked noose was dropped over the sobbing sailor's head. Winslow braced himself. Agonizing moments later an enormous gasp went up from the ships, and then a deathly calm shrouded them. The sailor's body swayed in the gulf breeze.

Chapter Four

An Ironic
Shipboard Meeting

To quiet the clamor at home, Navy Secretary George Bancroft sent Perry down to straighten out the mess. The pill was made more palatable both to Conner and congressmen when he was assigned command of the sailing ships, and Perry the steam vessels.

Winslow wrote Kathy that he was disgusted with war, that "vanity of courage and glory has no charm for me when I think of the misery and bleeding hearts that everywhere strew its tracks. I wonder how madmen become to be so ticked with emptiness ... I am no fighting man."

If Winslow was no fighting man, he certainly did not show it at Tabasco. The newspapers were delighted and the *New York Journal of Commerce* front-paged a stirring account of Winslow's heroism. Commodore Perry commended him publicly and made him master of the small Mexican sailing sloop, *Union*, one of the ships seized at Tabasco. The vessel was renamed the *Morris* in memory of Lieutenant C.W. Morris, who was killed by guerrilla fire during the expedition.

Winslow was elated at this, his first command, but quickly found that Perry had put a strange trust in him. Even the most experienced officer in the squadron would have found the *Morris* a tough ship to handle. She was completely without means of navigational aids, instruments, books, maps or lights. "And that stupid Perry refuses to issue me any of these things!" fumed Winslow who knew he would have a bear by the tail when the winter gales swept the gulf.

Winslow's fears came true two months later on the night of December 16, 1846, when a furious storm struck the fleet. Foamy breakers higher than his two-story house in Roxbury soon had the *Morris'* decks awash.

"We'll be alright," Winslow reassured the quartermaster, "if the *John Adams* doesn't change position." He knew that by keeping an eye on the lights of the *Adams*, which was serving as a makeshift lighthouse off the blacked out coast, he could always calculate his position. But the shrieking winds tore the *Adams* loose from her anchorage and she was blown far off her station.

Winslow grabbed the rail in the wheelhouse as a mountainous wave lifted the *Morris* and dropped her into another trough. "Watch those lights!" he cautioned, peering out into the storm-whipped darkness. The *Morris* keeled hard to starboard, nearly pitching him across the wheelhouse as the *Adams'* lights lured Winslow's ship to her doom. Her lead line suddenly snapped and was immediately lost. Seconds later the gale drove the *Morris* hard onto a reef. The jolting crash slammed Winslow against the bulkhead and cracked windows in the wheelhouse.

"Quick!" he shouted. "The anchor!" Winslow tried an old navigational trick. By drawing in on the anchor he might be able to pull the ship off the reef. Winslow felt the *Morris* begin to scrape across the rocks.

"Put on sail!" he yelled. "Put on sail! The wind'll blow us the rest of the way off!" With luck he'd save her.

"Now cut those anchor chains!" he shouted, barely

making himself heard over the howling wind. Winslow clung to the rail as his men bent against the gale and tried to batter through the chains.

"Harder, men! Harder!" The chains refused to part.

A huge wall of water rushed toward the *Morris*, shoved her off the reef for an instant, then scooped the tiny ship up and dropped her hard onto the rocks. Massive breakers filled one lifeboat and tore away another.

"Shall we abandon ship, sir," urged a crewman.

"Hell, no!"

"But we're breaking up!"

"Go if you wish, then," Winslow told his men. "I'm staying aboard!"

The *Morris* rocked violently under the battering of the waves. Winslow, alone and fighting to save his ship, heard the ocean's violent pounding. The *Morris* creaked from stem to stern.

"I'll put on sail to push her off the reef," Winslow muttered. But the storm buffeted her still harder, and when he saw chunks of the *Morris* washing overboard he realized further efforts to save her were suicidal. Winslow got clear just as she was pounded into driftwood by the waves.

Rescue boats from nearby ships quickly picked up Winslow and his men. Safe at last aboard the *USS Raritan* at Anton Lizarde, he took time to be miffed at Perry for failing to give him proper navigational gear. A board of inquiry hushed the incident by finding Winslow innocent.

While awaiting new orders, Winslow shared a cabin with another lieutenant who was also bemoaning the loss four months earlier of his first command, the brig *USS Somers* of notorious mutiny fame. A sudden squall had capsized her with heavy loss of life. He, too, was a native

Lt. Raphael Semmes, later an Admiral in the Confederate Navy, befriended Lt. John Winslow. They both had lost their ships. Later these friends would become enemies, as one fought for the North, and the other for the South.

southerner, was about Winslow's age, sparely built, of medium height and with piercing blue eyes which, while friendly, seemed to bore through Winslow. His name was Raphael Semmes.

The two young lieutenants tried to make light of their harrowing experiences in losing their first ships. "Winslow," said Semmes, "The Navy is going to send you out to learn the bearing of reefs," to which Winslow replied, "Raph, they're going to send *you* out to learn how to take care of your ship in a squall."

Tropic diseases struck Winslow, and despite his protests Perry sent him home to recuperate. He spent the rest of the war as ordnance officer at the Boston Navy Yard. Less than a year later new orders assigned him as executive officer aboard the sloop of war *USS Saratoga*. For the first time that Winslow could remember he truly regretted sea duty. He was 36-years-old and hated to leave home, his sons and daughters and Kathy who grew more beautiful with childbearing.

The monotonous cruise of the *Saratoga* did not help matters. Winslow realized that the poor pay and possibility of his death before he could adequately provide for his family was not the best lure for a naval career. How else, though, could he support them?

During Winslow's tedious hours he developed an idea that had occurred to him while he was aboard the *Missouri*. He built a model of his invention, a camel steam tug, and made plans to patent the idea. The tug could take ships over bars, however shallow they might be.

"New Orleans, Mobile, Savannah and Charleston could have the largest ships towed up to their wharves with as much facility as the common tow-boats now take the vessels out to deep water." Winslow enthusiastically told fellow officers. "The whole southern coastline which before this was shut because of bars would now be open for commerce. Just imagine how valuable my invention could be to the country!"

Everyone agreed with Winslow, including a British admiral who looked at the gadget. Winslow sent a miniature tugboat to the Navy Department where the tradition-bound oldtimers would have nothing to do with it.

"Their brains turned to sawdust 20 years ago," Winslow grumbled. "I'll show 'em. I'll sell it to the Russians. They could use my tug at St. Petersburg." He never got around to contacting Moscow, however.

Had the Navy paid attention to Winslow's invention, a great deal of trouble, ships and lives might have been spared during the Civil War. Perhaps, too, the war might have been shortened considerably. Because of the Confederacy's 3,000-mile coastline of sandbars and shoals, the Union blockaders could not make thrusts against many Rebel strongholds.

Winslow forgot his invention when the *Saratoga* returned to the United States and he enjoyed two years of shore duty. Shortly before Kathy was to become a mother again, he received orders to the frigate *USS St. Lawrence* that was fitting out at the New York Navy Yard for duty as flagship of the Pacific Station.

The following four years were the most distasteful of Winslow's career. Cruising duty during peacetime irritated him when he saw life pulsating everywhere around him while he sat out the best years of his life aboard a sleepy frigate. More than ever he realized that landlocked Roxbury offered a few comforts that his mistress, the sea, did not. Winslow's melancholia deepened when he learned of the death of the son Kathy bore him shortly after the *St. Lawrence* sailed.

The cruise finally ended, and Winslow might have quit the Navy had he not been promoted to commander, assigned to recruiting duty, and later appointed Inspector of the Second Light House District with headquarters in Boston. The man who signed his appointment was Semmes, new secretary of the Lighthouse Board.

Chapter Five

"Bag Old Abe, Too!"

Then came Fort Sumter, the initial battle of the Civil War.

Winslow and Semmes were expected to support the Confederacy. Semmes quit the board and hurried to Montgomery, Alabama, where he reported for duty to Provisional President Jefferson Davis.

Winslow remained loyal to the Union and asked for sea duty. Instead of the action he craved, he was sent to the malaria-ridden Mississippi to assist Captain Andrew Foote in outfitting the Union flotilla at Cincinnati for the imminent fight for control of the vital river.

Winslow never saw such confusion amid a conglomeration of alleged men-o'-war. Here was Mexico all over again. Seven ironclad gunboats were under construction. They were being encased by 2 1/2-inches of iron plating and armed with 15 guns. The wheelhouse stood in the center and was protected by inclined plates so shots would bounce off like ping pong balls on a tin roof.

To Winslow, reared in the old sailing Navy, these were hideous mountains of iron, and he wondered how President Lincoln could be so stupid as to permit construction of these cumbersome monstrosities. How, with their enormous weight, could the ironclads navigate the shallow Mississippi without getting stuck in the mud?

The attack which began the Civil War in earnest—firing on Fort Sumter, South Carolina, by secessionists on April 12, 1861.

Winslow took the flagship *USS Benton* on a trial run down river and cussed mightily when the gunboat went hard aground 30 miles south of St. Louis. He worked all night to free the iron turtle, but she only burrowed deeper into the mud. Half a dozen 11-inch hawsers were brought out the next day and ropes stretched from them to trees on the river bank. The steam capstans whined, the ropes went taut, and the *Benton* grunted while trying to pull herself free.

Winslow was supervising the operation from beside a hawser whose line led through a snatch-block fastened by a large chain to a ringbolt on the *Benton's* side. The chain suddenly snapped. Links whizzed past Winslow, and a chunk more than an inch in diameter sliced into his left arm just below the elbow, reamed out the muscle and dug down to the bone. He yelped with pain and fell to the deck, holding his gashed arm. The *Benton's* surgeon quickly applied a tourniquet, sewed Winslow's arm together, and ordered him home to recuperate.

Fort Sumter burns and is lost. The initial battle of the Civil War ended in a victory for the Confederates, who were determined to secede from the Union.

U.S.S. Benton, *a river ironclad, which Winslow commanded on her maiden voyage down the Mississippi River. The unwieldy boat ran aground, and during the operation to free her, Winslow was severely injured. When he was able to return to duty, he was promoted to Captain.*

Although his arm healed slowly, Winslow was anxious to return to duty so he might win himself a command, even if it might be one of these damnable ironclads. He reported back to the flotilla and was made skipper of the *Baron de Kalb*. On July 16, 1862, Winslow was promoted to Captain, an appointment he considered far out of proportion to his rather menial duties. He positively expected that responsibilities more commensurate with his rank would not be long in coming.

Winslow saw his opportunity coming sooner than he thought when the ailing Charles H. Davis was relieved of the flotilla's command. Winslow assumed he would replace Davis and was astounded when David D. Porter, a captain junior to Winslow, was appointed flag officer. To say Winslow

DAVID DIXON PORTER 1813 - 1891

Winslow resented Porter's promotion, and said so in a scathing letter to Navy Secretary Gideon Welles. Upon reading the letter, Welles relieved Winslow of duty and placed him on furlough. Winslow was stunned.

was miffed is putting it mildly. He determined to do something about it.

About this time Winslow learned the South had driven Major General John Pope's troops back to Arlington Heights, Virginia during the Second Battle of Bull Run. It was a miserable campaign of confusion by the Union Army leaders.

"I'm glad of it," Winslow commented to a reporter. "I wish the Rebs would bag Old Abe, too." Winslow was disgusted with the flustered conduct of the Mississippi River campaign, too, and he recalled the debacle off Vera Cruz.

Winslow made it plain he thought President Lincoln was a "chowderhead," and without hesitation told a newspaper reporter it would be a good thing for the country if Lincoln was taken prisoner by the Rebels, who were pushing close to the capital. And good riddance to him, too. "Until something drastic is done to arouse Washington we shall have no fixed policy," he said.

When Navy Secretary Gideon Welles and President Lincoln saw the story in the *Baltimore American* they were sorely irked at this unheard of blast by a mere naval captain. They did not throttle Winslow because they secretly admitted that much of what he said about the conduct of the war was true.

"Just wait," said Lincoln, "Give him enough rope and he'll hang himself." The time could not come too soon to suit Secretary Welles.

The Bad Boy of the Union Navy promptly proceeded to get himself in more hot water. A Confederate officer taken prisoner at Fort Donelson was given exceptionally good treatment by Winslow, who not only welcomed him aboard the *Baron de Kalb* but gave him a tour of the ironclads as

Union President Abraham Lincoln, whom Winslow called an "Old Chowderhead." Although the chowderhead story appeared in the Baltimore American, *and Lincoln read it, the long suffering Lincoln overlooked Winslow's scathing comments.*

well. Secretary Welles was astounded when he heard that Winslow had gone out of his way to show the prisoner some of the gunboat's weaknesses. "I'm all for charging this Rebel in a Union uniform with treason," he said.

Winslow's explanation did not sooth Welles or Lincoln, either. He pointed out that the prisoner had fought the gunboat at Donelson and therefore already knew her weak points. His sole purpose in showing the Rebel the inside of

Navy Secretary Gideon Welles was irked at Winslow's blast at Lincoln, but he deferred to Lincoln's advice: "Give him [Winslow] enough rope, and he'll hang himself."

the gunboat, said Winslow, was to impress upon him the fact that these weaknesses were being corrected.

Winslow's story might have sufficed and his unfriendly remarks about the commander-in-chief overlooked had not Winslow, still smarting over Porter's promotion, taken pen in hand to write Welles a scathing letter in which he intimated the department had double-crossed him by promoting Porter. Winslow's demands for a new assignment were not couched in language aimed at winning friends and influencing people.

"Outrageous!" bellowed Acting Rear Admiral Davis, who strongly suggested that Winslow's letter was a distinct act of insubordination and should be punished as such. Welles agreed and retaliated by placing Winslow on furlough, a sharp slap in the face when every available officer was needed at a time the south was racking up one victory after another.

Winslow, for some reason not readily apparent to him, was flabbergasted by his relief from duty. He returned to Roxbury both sick in heart and body. Lingering illnesses from the Mexican War were severely aggravated by malaria caught in the Mississippi swamps. Worse, a painful disease attacked his vision and he began to lose the sight of his right eye.

Welles might storm at the mention of Winslow's name, but it was a privilege he could not long afford to indulge himself. He would have to order Winslow back to duty. One thing seemed certain, however, and that was that Winslow must somehow be punished. He was a dangerous man to have around. Remarks like Winslow's could stir up trouble on the homefront.

Secretary Welles studied his operational plans and smiled. He found just the spot, a real lemon, and just the ship, a real bucket of bolts. Out towards Africa — as unlikely a scene for Civil War action as you could find — *somebody* had to watch for Rebel cruisers like the *USS Sumter* commanded by Captain Semmes that were burning and sinking Yankee merchantmen. Why not Winslow?

The smart-alecky captain could sit out the war until he rotted, pop off all he wanted, and nobody would hear him. Welles knew it was not patriotic to make light of such things, but he could not help chuckling over the headaches in store for Winslow when he took over his ship.

Early in December 1862, the bedridden Winslow received orders directing him to board the *USS Vanderbilt* for passage to Fayal in the Azores, where he was to relieve Captain Charles W. Pickering of the steam sloop *USS Kearsarge*. Welles promptly washed his hands of the loudmouthed captain, hopefully for the duration.

Winslow sourly realized he was being shipped out to left field, and the only compensating feature of the assignment was that he was getting command of an almost new steam and sailing ship. The *Kearsarge* was new alright, but as Winslow would soon discover, she was a disgrace to the fine New England art of shipbuilding and an everlasting shame upon Portsmouth, New Hampshire, where she was launched.

Although his doctor protested against his return to duty, Winslow would hear none of it, and he took a train for New York. Winslow very nearly missed his date with fame. Four miles from Springfield, Massachusetts, the two locomotives were barreling the train through heavy snows when the engines suddenly hurtled from the tracks and dragged three cars with them. He escaped injury but was too sick to leave his berth to see what had happened.

When Winslow arrived in Fayal the day before Christ-

U.S.S. Sumter, *commanded by Winslow's former friend, Captain Raphael Semmes. Semmes defected to the Confederate Navy.*

U.S.S. Kearsarge. *As punishment for Winslow, Secretary of War Welles assigned him to command the* Kearsarge. *Although new, she was deemed a disgrace to the shipbuilding profession. Welles ordered Winslow to sail her across the Atlantic. Arriving in Cadiz, France, after her maiden voyage, the new* Kearsarge *needed a major overhaul.*

mas, 1862, he learned there would be a slight delay in the *Kearsarge's* arrival, a delay which was to last nearly four months. It wasn't that Pickering wished to prolong his tour of duty aboard the *Kearsarge* or that he was tracking Semmes in the *Sumter*. Not at all. He was simply unable to sail her to Fayal where he was as eager to be rid of her and her lackadaisical crew as Winslow was to command her.

Pickering told the Navy Department what he thought of the white elephant foisted upon them by profiteering Yankee shipbuilders. Even against Semmes' unseaworthy *Sumter*, a converted steam packet, the *Kearsarge* ran a poor second. Almost from the day she was launched she needed repairs.

If Secretary Welles was counting upon the *Kearsarge* to catch Semmes, who so far had made prizes of 18 Yankee merchantmen, he was leaning upon a weak reed. The secretary had to hand it to Semmes: he was truly making goats of the captains of pursuing Yankee cruisers. Six ships had been drawn off the blockade to chase the *Sumter* but she had eluded every trap set for her. Semmes slipped past some of the best officers in the Navy, most of them more experienced than Winslow, and some of the fastest cruisers. It would not ruffle Welles' feeling if Semmes added Winslow to his list of also-rans.

Pickering put into Madeira and heard Semmes was bottled up at Gibraltar by several Yankee ships. He could do nothing to help them because the *Kearsarge* needed more repairs before he dared take her out. Pickering finally managed to get to sea but was quickly forced to head back to drydock again when the *Kearsarge* resumed her complaints. A board of survey took one look at her, threw up its hands in dismay, and pronounced her machinery unsafe. The board ordered the *Kearsarge* to Cadiz for a major overhaul. A major overhaul of her crew was in order, too. Their morale was at a low ebb.

The *Sumter* would never give Winslow cause for worry. Semmes abandoned his worn out ship at Gibraltar and headed for England, where he bided his time before sailing for Terceira in the Azores to take command of the sleek English-built *CSS Alabama.*

If Welles' cruisers found it difficult to catch up with the *Sumter,* they would find it impossible to see so much as the *Alabama's* wake. She was one of the fastest ships afloat and was ideal for wreaking hit-and-run havoc upon ships supplying the Union war effort. This, the *Alabama* promptly proceeded to do.

During the next 22 months Semmes ranged from New York to Singapore in high seas depradations that would

C.S.S. Alabama. *Confederate Naval Captain, Raphael Semmes, traded his sluggish* Sumter *for the* Alabama, *one of the fastest ships afloat. With it, he boarded 386 vessels, took 2,000 prisoners, and became the Civil War's most notorious pirate. It became Winslow's obsession with the cumbersome* Kearsarge, *to capture his former friend turned pirate.*

have made Winslow's Great Grandfather Rhett blanch. Semmes boarded 386 vessels, including 232 neutrals, took 2,000 prisoners, made prizes of 82 ships, and burned 52 of them. The value of his prizes was conservatively estimated at more than $6,000,000.

Semmes, elated by his easy victories over unarmed merchantmen, took to sporting a cocky pencil-thin moustache whose ends curled upwards at a jaunty angle. He kept the moustache so heavily waxed that his crewmen called him, "Old Beeswax" while cheering their captain as another helpless merchantman burned to her waterline.

Winslow meanwhile fidgeted impatiently in Fayal. He was shut off from the world by the remoteness of the island. Months passed and still the *Kearsarge* did not arrive. "Welles could have built another and sent it out here in the time it's taking to fix her," fumed Winslow as he spent days sweeping the horizon with his spyglass for some sign of the ship.

The *Kearsarge* finally puffed into Fayal. She was a bark-rigged sloop, and Winslow learned she was named after the New Hampshire mountains. He would soon learn, too, that she had a distinct tendency to handle like one.

During his first few weeks of cruising, Winslow attempted to learn more about the *Kearsarge* and tried hard to sympathize with her idiosyncracies. He spent even more time whipping his crew back to fighting trim. The crew's spirit soon revived.

On July 17, 1863, the blockade runner, *Juno*, blundered into Fayal while the *Kearsarge* was in port. The speedy little schooner took off like a frightened rabbit. Winslow set the cumbersome *Kearsarge* in pursuit, but she stumbled over her own anchor, and her journals ran hot. Winslow finally slipped his anchor chain and prodded the *Kearsarge* into loping in the disappearing wake of the *Juno*. He caught up with the blockade runner four days later near Angra and took her captive.

When Winslow brought the *Kearsarge* back to Fayal he found that someone had cut the buoy rope marking the spot where he had abandoned his anchor in his haste to chase the *Juno*. Winslow gave over the next two days to dragging for it and cursed the English consul whom he was positive had ordered the rope cut in retaliation for catching the *Juno*, which was carrying British supplies to the Confederacy.

When the *CSS Florida* was reported near the coast of Ireland, considerably off the *Kearsarge's* track, Winslow pointed her bowsprit northwards as a strategy occurred to him. He damned "those alleged brains in the Navy Department" for not thinking of it sooner.

Winslow realized he might conceivably search the seas for months and still not sight a Rebel cruiser's sails. Did it not stand to reason, then, that he would have a better chance of spotting one by concentrating in the locality from which they came and where they would have to return to refuel and replenish their provisions? What this amounted to was a blockade of Europe, specifically the area where the English Channel meets the Atlantic Ocean.

Lincoln would object to the idea of a potential international incident, but to hell with him. Secretary Welles, too. Winslow had been at sea almost a year, and nobody had bothered to inquire about his activities or to suggest the cruising area. It was enough for Winslow that nobody told him he *could not* mosey up to England and France.

Winslow's plan worked admirably. For the time being, anyway. He caught up with the *CSS Florida* at Brest and promptly blockaded her. When Winslow learned the *Florida* would be in port for a month undergoing repairs, he asked the Navy Department to send him some cruisers to help block the three channels leading from Brest. The Navy ignored the request, and the French emperor, Napoleon II, whose sympathies were with the Confederacy, made it obvious he wished Winslow would put lots of open sea between Brest and the *Kearsarge.*

Winslow gladly obliged him, but only after receiving word from U.S. Minister James E. Harvey at Lisbon that the *CSS Georgia* was on her way up the English Channel, probably en route to Cherbourg. Winslow set out for Cherbourg, but a channel gale pounded the *Kearsarge* so badly he put into Queenstown, Ireland, for repairs. In light of what was about to happen, Winslow probably would have preferred the savagery of the storm.

The night the *Kearsarge* sailed from Queenstown, 16 stowaways were discovered. They insisted upon joining Winslow's crew, but he realized such enlistments were distinct violations of English neutrality and promptly put them ashore.

The episode would have been forgotten had not the incident exploded four months later into a violent attack upon Winslow. The Earl of Donoughmore stood up in the House of Lords and sputtered that the United States was violating British neutrality. He said Winslow's sworn statement that he was unaware the crewmen were aboard until he got to sea contradicted depositions made by the men themselves, who claimed they were coaxed into joining the Union Navy.

In short, Winslow was a liar. Moreover, the Marquis de Clanricarde objected to allowing the *Kearsarge* to be repaired in Her Majesty's Queenstown shipyard.

Winslow was infuriated over the tempest and wrote a long open letter to the marquis which Winslow released to British newspapers. In effect, Winslow told the marquis he was a muttonhead and besides, even if the law allowed, the *Kearsarge* would not have deigned to enlist "such miserable English scum as those who secreted themselves the night I put to sea."

It's doubtful the marquis was mollified by Winslow's sarcastic explanation, just as certain as it is that this unprecedented debut of a naval officer into the field of international diplomacy was a miserable flop.

"A proceeding of this kind is wholly irregular," snapped U.S. Consul Charles Francis Adams when he saw the newspapers. Irregular was hardly the word for it. Although Winslow was later vindicated, the letter blossomed into a full-blown international incident. Adams told Winslow: "I feel it is my duty to make a report of this matter to Mr. Lincoln.

"Nuts!" said Winslow.

Chapter Six

On the Track
of the Alabama

Navy Secretary Welles and President Lincoln, who thought they had heard the last of their Bad Boy, were shocked when they heard Winslow had suddenly turned up off the coast of England.

Welles summed up his own and Lincoln's reaction when he wrote Winslow to henceforth keep his mouth shut and leave the diplomatic wars to professionals. If it was fighting Winslow wanted, why had he not done something about Semmes, who was continuing to make dunces of the Navy brass! The New York Chamber of Commerce was storming at the White House, and Lincoln was demanding that the Navy end the *Alabama's* piracy.

Winslow dourly continued to prowl the channel. The *Kearsarge* was like a cat watching two mouse holes on either side of the pantry. The *Florida* was nearly repaired at Brest and promising to make a dash for freedom almost any day. The *Georgia* was at Cherbourg. Winslow heard that Semmes was somewhere close by, too. To add to his troubles, a new Rebel cruiser, the *CSS Rappahannock,* suddenly appeared in Calais.

What was Winslow going to do about all this, asked the U.S. Consul's office in Paris. "Tell that fool Welles to send me some help," Winslow shot back. "I can't be everywhere at once." Old Gideon wasn't listening, however. Winslow had made his bed, now let him sleep in it.

When Winslow dropped down to Cadiz for supplies and coal, the unpredictable French suddenly gave the two Rebel cruisers orders to leave port within 24 hours. They did not know, nor little cared, that Winslow had temporarily left his blockading station in the channel. He was crestfallen when he returned and saw his two prime catches had escaped.

Winslow felt like an orphan in the stormy waters of the English Channel now whipped to foamy fury by winter gales. Mere mention of Winslow's name was certain to put Lincoln in a tizzy. Welles hated Daniel Webster and Matthew Perry for forcing him on the Navy. The French made it plain they could do without Winslow's company, and the English were positive he would never darken their newspaper columns again.

Winslow continued to lie in wait for Rebel cruisers. He realized the *Rappahannock* would easily escape, too, if the *Kearsarge* put in for badly needed repairs to Belgium, one of the few remaining havens he dared try. Winslow thought his luck had changed when the French, wearying of the *Rappahannock's* presence, seized her. Then, in typical French fashion, they debated whether or not to return her to the Rebels. Winslow could not wait for the emperor to make up his mind. He had to get the *Kearsarge* into drydock before she drowned in her own juice.

Winslow chartered the steamer *Annette* to stand by off Brest while he ran up to Ostend for repairs. If he expected a royal welcome from Belgium, Winslow was in for a surprise. As the *Kearsarge* put into the harbor, the Belgian pilot gave her too much sheet. The *Kearsarge* fouled a smack and carried away her topmast.

"Put the helm hard over," the pilot ordered. It was a wise move. But he kept the helm there too long.

"Look out, damn you!" yelled Winslow as the *Kearsarge* headed for the eastern side of the canal, a pedestrian bridge, and a pier. It was too late to stop the careening sloop. She wiped out the bridge, plowed into the pier, and ran up onto the beach, putting her forefoot high out of the water.

Winslow allowed as how he could have done a better job blindfolded of bringing in his problem child, and promptly directed guys to be got out from the mastheads and stayed by pennant tackles to keep the ship on an even keel until he could heave her off the beach at high tide. Winslow was positive the pilot's act was deliberate sabotage, but he could never prove it. The *Kearsarge* sulked off to Flushing, Holland, for repairs to her bruised bottom.

Similar problems were facing Semmes. The *Alabama* had been to sea nearly two years and was badly in need of drydock work. Sea water had corroded much of her copper bottom. In places the metal was so thin it had loosened and fallen off. The fires in her boilers had rarely been permitted to go out so the engineers could clink her bars and remove heavy incrustations of salt.

Semmes had no other choice but to take a breather and put in to a friendly port, say Brest or Cherbourg. No, Brest was out. The *Florida's* long stay had worn out the Confederacy's welcome. So were English ports out of the question. Where, then? Winslow was at anchor in the Scheldt River off Flushing on Sunday afternoon, June 12, 1864, when he received a telegram from William L. Dayton, U.S. Minister to Paris. The *Alabama* had dropped anchor in Cherbourg.

The Alabama had been at sea for two years and was badly in need of repair. Semmes headed for Cherbourg and destiny. Winslow and the Kearsarge were there waiting.

Winslow hoisted the *Kearsarge's* cornet and fired a signal gun calling all hands back from shore leave. Her fires were lit, and before nightfall the *Kearsarge's* bow was biting into the channel waters as she raced for France. On Tuesday afternoon Winslow steamed past the Cherbourg breakwater and stopped near the *Alabama*. The crews of the two ships crowded the rails and silently studied each other.

Perhaps never had two ships been so closely matched. They looked alike both in silhouette and deck layouts. The *Kearsarge* displaced 1,031 tons, the *Alabama*, 1,016. Winslow had a complement of 163 officers and men, Semmes, 149. Both ships were fairly new.

Winslow saw what Semmes meant when he described the *Alabama* as "sitting on the water with the lightness and grace of a swan." Like the *Kearsarge* she was a barkentine-rigged ship. Her long lower masts enabled her to carry large fore-and-aft jibs and try-sails for greater speed. The *Alabama's* engines could deliver 300 horsepower. To conserve her coal supply she could in 15 minutes hoist her propeller into a well high enough out of water so as not to be a drag on her excellent sailing speed of better than 13 knots.

The ships were also closely matched in battery. Winslow could deliver a 366-pound broadside; Semmes, 296, although the Alabama had one more gun than the *Kearsarge*. Winslow would rely upon her four broadside 32-pounders, a pair of 11-inch Dahlgren guns and one 28-pound rifle. Semmes had one 100-pound rifle with one heavy 68-pounder and six 32-pounders in broadside.

Although their armament and size were similar, Semmes would have to be supremely confident of victory to put his converted India merchantman against a ship expressly designed for war. Consequently, Winslow hardly expected the contemptuous challenge hurled by Semmes:

The officers of the Kearsarge. They lined the rails and studied their counterparts aboard the Confederate pirate ship Alabama which had pulled along side prior to the fierce battle between the two ships.

"My intention is to fight the *Kearsarge* as soon as I can make the necessary arrangements. I hope these will not deter me more than until tomorrow evening, or after the morrow morning at the furthest. I beg she will not depart before I am ready to go out."

Indeed Winslow would not.

The *Kearsarge* steamed out of Cherbourg and took up her station on blockade. The decks were cleared for action, and Winslow ordered a dress rehearsal for what was to come. Guns were run out, loaded, aimed, and practice fired. At Ostend, Winslow had noticed how the *Kearsarge's* bow withstood the terrific wallop. Winslow figured he might attempt to ram the *Alabama*, and so he ordered special drills at repelling boarders.

Earlier, Winslow had draped 120 fathoms of spare sheet chains for 49 1/2 feet alongside the *Kearsarge* to deflect shot and protect her boilers in case of a close-range fight. The chains hung in bights and were bolted down in conformity with the ship's contours, so the enemy could not see them.

Semmes ordered an extra 100 tons of coal put into the *Alabama's* bunkers so she would ride lower in the water and make a smaller target for Winslow.

Friday came and went. The *Alabama* did not come out as Semmes promised. Saturday passed. Still no *Alabama*. Winslow wondered whether Semmes might be losing his nerve.

Sunday, June 19, 1864, dawned bright and clear. Winslow gazed across the water from his station three miles north-northeast of the Cherbourg breakwater. The gentle breeze from the west barely ruffled the calm sea. He could not ask for better fighting weather.

Winslow felt certain the *Alabama* would not come out to fight today, either. Semmes would be downright foolish to pick weather like this which favored the *Kearsarge,* and Winslow knew his former messmate was no fool. More than likely Semmes probably realized the bluster of his challenge and planned to slip out of Cherbourg under cover of darkness, fog, or stormy seas.

It was 10 a.m. Captain Winslow made his routine Sunday inspection. The crew stood smartly at attention in their clean uniforms. Their lockers were neat, and the decks had been holystoned to a gleaming brightness. Below, the boilers throbbed at half-steam. Winslow was satisfied the *Kearsarge* and her crew were as close to fighting perfection as he could make them.

"Pipe the call for church services," said Winslow. After days of impatient waiting for Semmes to make good his threat, the tension was wearing off.

Winslow was in the middle of the service when the chief quartermaster on the bridge lifted his telescope and focused it on the entrance to the Cherbourg breakwater. Winslow saw him looking at the speck but continued to read. Executive Officer James S. Thornton quietly got up and went to the bridge.

Thornton saw a steam yacht flying the white British ensign come out and stand to the northward. He returned to his chair. The quartermaster continued to focus his telescope on the breakwater for several minutes, then hurried down the port gangway until he was close behind the worshippers. To make sure of what he'd seen, the quartermaster looked once more toward Cherbourg.

"She's coming!" he yelled.

Chapter Seven

The Last Battle
of the Woodenclads

"Amen!" said Winslow, ending the service in the middle of a sentence. Putting aside his prayerbook, he stepped to the rail and took the quartermaster's glass. There was no doubt about it. The *Alabama* was coming out to fight.

"Mr. Thornton, Winslow said quietly. "Beat to quarters." The steady roll of drums sent excitement pulsating through the *Kearsarge*.

The ship was cleared for action, the decks sanded to soak up blood, the battery pivoted to starboard. Winslow ordered the *Kearsarge* to steam six to seven miles out to sea. If Semmes got his nose bloodied, Winslow did not want to give him the opportunity of slipping back inside the safety of the three-mile limit. Too, the additional sailing time would allow the *Kearsarge's* boilers to build a full head of steam.

"Don't fail me now," Winslow begged the *Kearsarge* as he went to his cabin, took off his cap and put on the battered one he kept for use in foul weather.

Winslow went back on deck and climbed up onto the horse-block abreast of the mizzen mast, close the starboard bulwarks. Although half of his heavy-set body stood above the rail and would afford *Alabama* sharpshooters a perfect target, this spot would give him a commanding view of the battle and put him within easy speaking trumpet contact with his quartermaster, the officer at the engine hatch bell, and Thornton who would direct the batteries.

It was now 10:50, half an hour since the quartermaster descried the *Alabama*. Winslow ordered the *Kearsarge* to come about. He pointed her bow for the *Alabama's* and signaled full steam ahead. A plume of charcoal-grey smoke gushed from the *Kearsarge's* stack as she rushed headon toward the *Alabama* a mile and a quarter away.

"I expect she'll fire first," Winslow told Thornton. "Her guns have the range over ours, though we've got the heavier broadside. That won't do Semmes much good, however, if we can close in to get a few whacks at him."

The gap between the *Kearsarge* and the *Alabama* lessened.

Winslow and his men who had had no contact with shore since getting Semmes' challenge were the last to learn the *Alabama* planned to fight that day. Semmes' intentions of fighting on Sunday had been known for 48 hours in Cherbourg. Word of the impending fight had been flashed to Paris. Weekend excursion trains to the Cherbourg resort areas were crowded as entire families headed for picnic outings to watch the high seas melodrama.

Some of the curious brought camp stools to make themselves more comfortable while the fight between the two American ships was fought. Peddlers sold cheap binoculars at outrageous prices. The more fortunate — or possibly the more foresighted — had brought telescopes to get a better view of the action, certain to be a bloody one. Others could identify the two ships only by the black smoke trail left by the *Kearsarge*, which was burning bituminous coal from Newcastle. The *Alabama's* anthracite came from

Welsh mines and was giving off little smoke.

Betting was brisk among the mob of 19,000 lining escarpments, the mole, the heights, and the shoreline where a circus atmosphere prevailed. Sailors hung from the ratlines of men-o'-war and merchantmen in Cherbourg harbor. The odds favored the *Alabama*. With the inferior *Sumter*, Semmes had already sunk one Yankee warship and that one a vessel twice as heavy as the Rebel in men, armament, and was several knots faster, too. Some of the watchers were solemn. They had, a few weeks earlier, lost their ships and their worldly goods to Semmes, and were destitute in France until passage money arrived from home.

The ships were now a mile apart. The *Alabama* slowed, then sheered to port. Puffs of smoke shot from her starboard battery. Winslow felt the broadside whistle high over the *Kearsarge*. A foretopmast backstay snapped like a fiddlestring.

"Hold your fire, Mr. Thornton," said Winslow. "Steady as you go," he signaled the engineercom.

Again the *Alabama* yawed, and her guns spewed a second broadside of solid shot at 1,800 yards. More of the *Kearsarge's* rigging parted.

"Short range, Mr. Thornton," said Winslow reminding his executive that the *Kearsarge's* battery was loaded with 5-second shells. Semmes knew what Winslow was up to, but he feared a fight at close range. So long as the *Alabama* could keep her distance she would have the advantage. Winslow gave up his plan of ramming and boarding her. A lucky shot from the *Alabama* could rake his decks.

"Sheer to port!" Winslow trumpeted to his quartermaster. The *Kearsarge* drew off the *Alabama's* bow and took a third broadside for her trouble.

With 19,000 spectators lining the shore of the French resort area at Cherbourg, the Kearsarge and the Alabama opened fire on each other. Union Naval Captain Winslow was determined to stop his former friend turned pirate, Confederate Naval Captain Raphael Semmes.

"The range if you please, Mr. Thornton!" called Winslow The executive relayed the order to the crew at the 28-pound rifle on the forecastle. The *Kearsarge* trembled when the gun leaped back in recoil.

"Fire at your pleasure!" said Winslow as the *Kearsarge* stood 900 yards abreast of the *Alabama*. "But make sure of your aim. Heavy guns shoot below her waterline. Lighter ones clear her decks."

The *Kearsarge* drew blood with her first broadside. A 32-pound shell burst through the port of the *Alabama's* forward pivot gun, crushed the leg of a tackleman, caromed off the slide rack, and shredded a man at another gun.

Winslow calmly motioned the quartermaster to port the helm. He planned to run under the *Alabama's* stern, rake her, then range up her port side. Semmes was too fast for him. He quickly put his helm hard to port, and the two ships laid their track of battle by circling each other at full speed on opposite headings, a quarter to a half mile apart.

"He's got to fight now!" muttered Winslow, biting his lower lip in concentration. "Old Beeswax can't straighten out and head for shore without getting raked."

Semmes changed from solid shot to shell. The *Alabama* fired rapidly, two broadsides for every one got off by the deliberate gunners aboard the *Kearsarge*.

"Thank God their aim is rotten," said Winslow. "Only their after-pivot seems to have found the range. Something is wrong with their powder, too. It doesn't have the sock it should." Winslow saw that the hours he spent drumming gunnery into his men was paying off. While the *Alabama's* shots were erratic, the marvelous discipline of the *Kearsarge's* gunners made nearly every shot count. Her crew was performing like veterans, although for most of them this was their baptism of battle.

Again the *Kearsarge's* starboard broadside spurted flame. A shell tore away the *Alabama's* spanker gaff, and her flag fluttered to her deck. The gaff swung downward momentarily, then crashed in a tangled skein of running rigging. The *Kearsarge's* crewmen cheered. Semmes ran up another ensign as the *Alabama's* crew replied in kind. A shell ripped a gaping hole in the *Kearsarge's* spanker sail.

Another *Alabama* broadside. A 100-pound shell crashed into the *Kearsarge* amidships. Now it was the *Alabama's* turn to cheer. They thought their shot had penetrated the *Kearsarge's* boilers. Thanks to the chain plate it was deflected, and the shell passed harmlessly through the engineroom skylight. The *Alabama's* 100-pound rifle roared again. This time the *Kearsarge* reeled from the impact: the hardest jolt yet.

"Mr. Thornton!" said Winslow. "See what damage that one did!" While the executive ran aft, a shell from the *Alabama's* 68-pound Blakely gun ripped through the *Kearsarge's* starboard bulwarks, tore away more rigging, and exploded on the quarterdeck. When the smoke cleared, Winslow saw three crewmen sprawled on the deck. The sand was soaking up their blood. One was dying. Another was holding his broken thigh, and the third sat staring mutely at his badly mangled right arm that would have to be amputated.

"Take those men below!" said Winslow.

"That's alright, sir," the one with the broken arm called up to him. "We can make it ourselves." Winslow watched incredulously as the three crawled toward the forehatch.

Thornton returned. "We were lucky, sir. There's a 100-pound shell lodged in our sternpost just below the counter. If she'd have exploded we'd be on our way to Davy Jones. Must be the *Alabama's* powder has deteriorated."

Winslow felt the *Kearsarge* rock as another 100-pounder exploded in her smokestack, tearing an enormous gash in it. Two more shots bored through ports along the battery of 32-pounders and set fire to the hammock netting.

"Sound the alarm for fire quarters," bellowed Winslow. Hoses were run out and the flames were soon doused.

The *Kearsarge* stormed back. Her broadsides pounded the *Alabama* viciously. Winslow, squinting through his telescope, saw jagged holes being gouged out of the enemy's hull. Then a shell scored a direct hit on the *Alabama's* 32-pound after-port gun: the one which had been doing so much damage to the *Kearsarge*. It was a lucky shot, but battles are won on such things.

The shell burst slaughtered or injured every one of the 32-pounder's crew. Midshipman Anderson caught the full brunt and was blown to pieces. A powder-blackened *Alabama* crewman grabbed a coal scuttle and shoveled the grisly mess overboard.

"Mr. Thornton!" shouted Winslow over the tumult. "Aim a trifle more below her waterline."

The *Kearsarge* heaped one deadly broadside after another into the enemy as the 11-inch Dahlgrens punched holes below the Alabama's waterline and made a shambles of her spar deck. A shell bored through her hull and exploded in the engineroom. The *Alabama* shuddered from stem to stern. Seawater gushing into her engineroom, put out her fires and flooded the hold beyond the control of the pumps.

The two ships were finishing their seventh circle and were less than 500 yards apart. Winslow swept the *Alabama* with his telescope and saw she was severely hulled between the main and mizzen masts and settling by the stern. He decided to cross her stern and move in for the kill by raking her decks.

The Alabama takes on water and begins to founder.

"Stand by with the grape," Winslow told Thornton.

Semmes anticipated the move and shifted his helm as if to head for shore.

"Starboard the helm!," signaled Winslow. The *Kearsarge* passed under the *Alabama's* stern and ranged up her port side. He saw that her head sails were set to pay off on a new tack, but she was settling and answering her rudder sluggishly.

Again the *Kearsarge's* broadsides pounded the *Alabama*. Her shots tore gaping new holes below the waterline and sent geysers of water high into the air. Semmes could bring only two 32-pounders to bear. He sent his executive officer, John Kell, below to see how much longer the *Alabama* could stay afloat. When he got Kell's report that she was sinking fast, Semmes struck his colors.

The officers of the Kearsarge *admire their well-polished gun that is credited with sending the Alabama to the bottom of Cherbourg Harbour.*

73

"She's ours!" beamed Winslow. His crew cheered and threw their caps into the air. But there was confusion aboard the *Alabama*. Two young lieutenants refused to quit and her port guns fired again.

"Those sneaking bastards," stormed Winslow. "Let 'em have another!" The *Kearsarge* returned the broadside and steamed into a raking position across the *Alabama's* bows. A white flag flew from her stern, and the ensign was half-masted, union down.

Winslow studied the sinking ship with his glass. Semmes was no longer on his horse-block and now stood alongside the rail. He threw his sword into the water as the Rebel crewmen took to their lifeboats. A quarter-boat started to pull for the *Kearsarge* with a Confederate officer and 20 wounded men aboard.

"Does Captain Semmes surrender his ship?" Winslow called down to them.

"Yes," replied the officer. Winslow again looked at the *Alabama*. Semmes was leaping into the water.

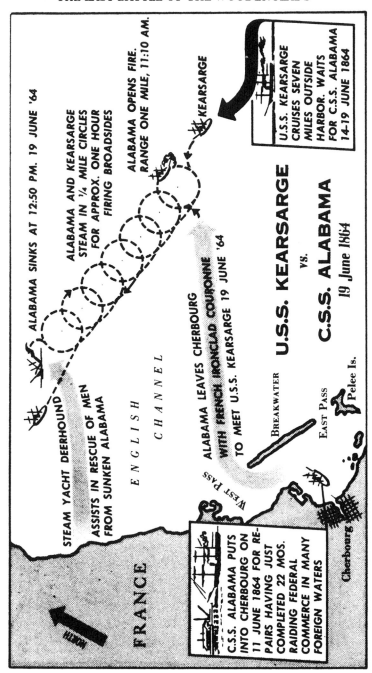

U.S.S. KEARSARGE CRUISES SEVEN MILES OUTSIDE HARBOR. WAITS FOR C.S.S. ALABAMA 14-19 JUNE 1864

KEARSARGE

ALABAMA SINKS AT 12:50 PM. 19 JUNE '64

ALABAMA AND KEARSARGE STEAM IN ¼ MILE CIRCLES FOR APPROX. ONE HOUR FIRING BROADSIDES

ALABAMA OPENS FIRE. RANGE ONE MILE, 11:10 AM.

STEAM YACHT DEERHOUND ASSISTS IN RESCUE OF MEN FROM SUNKEN ALABAMA

ENGLISH CHANNEL

ALABAMA LEAVES CHERBOURG WITH FRENCH IRONCLAD COURONNE TO MEET U.S.S. KEARSARGE 19 JUNE '64

U.S.S. KEARSARGE vs. C.S.S. ALABAMA

19 June 1864

BREAKWATER

EAST PASS

Pelee Is.

WEST PASS

C.S.S. ALABAMA PUTS INTO CHERBOURG ON 11 JUNE 1864 FOR RE-PAIRS HAVING JUST COMPLETED 22 MOS. RAIDING FEDERAL COMMERCE IN MANY FOREIGN WATERS

Cherbourg

FRANCE

NORTH

75

Chapter Eight

A Bittersweet
Hero's Welcome

The *Kearsarge* was virtually powerless to rescue the Alabama's crewmen, whose heads were bobbing in the ocean swells. Winslow found three of his lifeboats were shattered, and only two others serviceable, the sailing launch and the second cutter, both of them hard to reach, however. The English yacht, *Deerhound*, that preceded the Alabama from Cherbourg hurried over to the *Kearsarge* and offered her help.

"For God's sake do what you can to save them!" Winslow called down to the *Deerhound*. The yacht darted among the drowning crewmen of the Alabama and saved many, as did boats from a French ironclad frigate, the *Couronne*. Winslow finally got his boats away, and they joined in the rescue work.

At 24 minutes past noon, an hour and 27 minutes after the battle started, the bow of the shattered and bloody *Alabama* rose high, almost perpendicularly out of the water. Her fore and main masts snapped and fell overboard. Then the *Alabama* shot straight to the bottom in 45 fathoms, dragging with her many wounded crewmen. As the water swallowed her, an immense whirlpool sucked many more of them under.

Winslow watched solemnly as the last of the *Alabama's* bubbles came up. Thornton called his attention to the *Deerhound,* which was steaming off toward England with a full load of survivors. "Semmes is aboard her," said Thornton. "I saw him."

"The *Deerhound* will be back." said Winslow confidently. "She's simply coming 'round." But the *Deerhound* continued to open the gap between herself and the *Kearsarge.*

"I tell you, sir, she's escaping with Semmes!" insisted Thornton.

"Impossible!" She wouldn't steam away without first communicating with me. No Englishman carrying the flag of the Royal Yacht Squadron could do such a thing as help prisoners of the United States Navy escape."

Winslow was in for a rude jolt. The *Deerhound* did *not* stop until she reached Liverpool, where Semmes was treated as the victor. The Queenstown past of the Bad Boy of the Union Navy had caught up with Winslow. He stormed that the *Deerhound* was hired as the *Alabama's* consort, a point Winslow was never able to prove.

Except for the escape of Semmes, which tarnished Winslow's superb naval victory, he might have become as immortalized as the two Civil War Davids: Farragut and Porter. Winslow pouted that it was quite unsporting of Semmes to surrender his ship and not himself, too. But Old Beeswax could hardly be blamed for escaping when he knew a hangman's noose awaited him in the United States if he was taken prisoner. The North never caught Semmes until after the war when he was arrested, jailed and later pardoned by President Andrew Johnson.

Despite Semmes' escape, Winslow was warmly welcomed back to the United States on the eve of a presidential

Confederate States Navy Admiral Raphael Semmes shouted his surrender to Winslow, but then leaped off of the Alabama *into the harbor, and was rescued by the* Deerhound. *Semmes escaped to fight another day.*

A detailed account of Semmes leading a subsequent Civil War battle on land is recounted in Part II of this book.

election. Lincoln and Welles made it obvious that all was forgiven. The president was pleased to be able to report to the terrified New England shipowners and the New York Chamber of Commerce that "Semmes the Pirate has finally been scourged from the seas." It helped to clinch Lincoln's reelection.

If Winslow was politically minded, he probably would have enjoyed the adulation. Old Gideon did himself proud by delivering an oration in which he congratulated Winslow for a victory, "over a vessel superior in tonnage, superior in number of guns, and superior in the number of her crew. The battle was so brief," intoned Welles, "the victory so decisive, and the comparative results so striking, that the country will be reminded of the brilliant actions of our infant Navy ..."

Historians have not recorded Winslow's reactions to Welles' testimonial, and even if they had, it's doubtful they would be printable. Suffice it to say, the *Kearsarge* steamed into Boston Harbor after nightfall on November 7, 1864, as the Civil War drew to a close. It was enough for Winslow that he was home at last to Kathy.

Roxbury applauded their returning hero and presented him with an ornate silver service. Three days later a public reception was held in Boston's Fanueil Hall for Winslow, who sat dourly through another parade, speechmaking and drinking of toasts. The city's merchants subscribed a $21,000 gift, and the New York Chamber of Commerce gave him $25,000.

Winslow heard that the president — "Old Abe the Chowderhead" — was asking Congress to recommend a vote of thanks. Lincoln said he would match it by promoting Winslow to commodore.

JOHN ANCRUM WINSLOW
1811 - 1873

*All of Winslow's past misdeeds were forgiven when he returned
to Boston Harbor after sinking the Alabama across the Atlantic. Lincoln, whom Winslow had called "Old Chowderhead,"
asked Congress to recommend a note of thanks, and promoted
him to Commodore.*

Epilogue

When the war ended a few months later, Winslow was put in command of the Gulf Squadron. Within two years the Bad Boy of the Union Navy was in hot water again.

During a meeting in New Orleans of the pre-Northern group, the Convention of 1864, changes in the state's government were suggested. The defeated Rebels objected strongly, and the convention hall was stormed by a mob. In the riot which followed, 40 persons were killed and nearly 150 wounded.

"I'm not going to take any guff from these Johnny Rebs," raged Winslow, disregarding the fact that he, himself, was a Johnny Reb of sorts. Winslow mobilized his ironclads and was set to flatten New Orleans if his heavily-armed landing force did not stomp out the riot. Before they went ashore, however, troops quelled the disturbance.

Secretary Welles indignantly criticized Winslow when he heard what the commodore almost did to New Orleans. This was no way to treat a beaten enemy. Hadn't anyone impressed upon Winslow the meaning of Grant's compassion at Appomattox?

"Panty-waisted politician!" snorted Winslow.

Peace was eventually restored in the Navy family, and Winslow was assigned to the Portsmouth Navy Yard. On March 2, 1870, he was promoted to Rear Admiral and given command of the Pacific Station. He got special permission from the Navy Department to take Kathy and his youngest daughter along with him.

Two years later Winslow suffered a stroke several minutes after stepping from his bath, and never fully recovered from the paralysis. He resigned his command and recuperated a year in California before heading home. Winslow got as far as New York City, where he suffered another attack in the lobby of the Old Ebbitt House while he was sending his baggage off to Roxbury. When he recovered sufficiently to travel he went home, where he died September 29, 1873.

In accord with her husband's final wishes, Kathy refused a military funeral. Simple services were held in St. James Episcopal Church. The *Kearsarge's* battle flag was draped over his coffin, and he was buried in Forest Hill Cemetery. Winslow's grave is marked by a granite boulder from the Kearsarge Mountains.

PART II

ADMIRAL SEMMES ON LAND:

THE
GREAT TRAIN ROBBERY
OF THE
CIVIL WAR

ADMIRAL RAPHAEL SEMMES
1809 - 1877

With his Rebel navy trapped in Richmond, and a hangman's noose awaiting him when the Yankees took over the city, Admiral Raphael Semmes hatched a desperate plan — one in keeping with his reputation as a pirate. He captured a railroad train and christened it the *Alabama II!*

The ragged column of Confederate sailors, led by the tall and lean admiral, hurried through the smoking streets toward the teeming mass of people swarming around the Richmond & Danville Railroad depot. A squad of cavalrymen, their horses kicking up swirling clouds of dust, galloped past.

"Hey, Admiral!" shouted one of the riders, reining his horse, "When d'y'all expect to drop anchor in Fort Warren!"

"How does the Admiral like navigatin' on land?" another cavalryman called out.

Rear Admiral Raphael Semmes, late of the Confederacy's commerce raiders *Sumter* and *Alabama*, wiped the sweat and grime from his face and smoothed back the heavily beeswaxed ends of his mustache. The proudly erect seafarer didn't like it one bit, but he'd be damned if he'd give this young upstart the satisfaction of knowing how he felt.

Semmes forced a smile and admitted there was an element of comedy in this, the calamity at Richmond, shortly after 7:30 that sunny spring morning of Monday, April 3, 1865. His were as disheveled a bunch of infantrymen as the Confederacy had ever fielded. Semmes' colonels, who only 24 hours earlier were Navy captains and still wore the braid to prove it, were trying to mold the motley column of 500 sailors into some semblance of a military file.

They were a ludicrous sight, loaded down with pots and pans, mess kettles, bags of bread, chunks of salted pork, sugar, tea, tobacco, and cutty pipes. Semmes knew they were fish out of water. Their port-to-starboard-and-back-again rolling cadence didn't augur much of a future for them as infantrymen. The Admiral knew they couldn't march a dozen miles before the heftiest salts fell under the weight of their packs.

"Seeing as how this is a railroad town," Semmes told his chief boatswain, "our only hope is to get a train out of here." Judging from the hollow rumbling of the distant cannon wheels and the jubilant shouts of the enemy as the vanguard of Grant's Union Army poured into burning Richmond, Semmes realized the city would be overwhelmed by Yankees within the hour; he'd have to move fast if he hoped to find transportation, assuming there was some. For his sailors, capture meant Libby Prison. Not so with Semmes. There was a price on his head that would make any Yankee soldier a rich man, because the North was itching to hang Semmes as a pirate in retaliation for his sea raids against New England shipping. Semmes knew his life depended upon him reaching the new Confederate capital at Danville, where he could regroup his naval forces with Lee's army.

The R&D Railroad station was a shouting bedlam of frenzied men rushing about wildly, women sobbing their despair, and shrieking children. Confederate wounded hobbled on crutches, some dazed, others forlorn.

"Who's in charge here?" Semmes asked a weasel-faced brakeman in oil-spotted overalls.

"How should I know? I sure as hell ain't!"

"Well, then, where can I find your superintendent?"

"Y'all ain't a-goin' to! He highballed outta here at dawn. Took most of the brass with 'im, along with Jeff Davis and the rest of the government officials. Their books 'n papers took up so much room there warn't space for any of us to squeeze aboard, so they left us behind."

Semmes couldn't believe it. Was it possible that he and his men had been abandoned by the Confederacy and left to escape from Richmond as best they could? What a plum for the Yankees: The South's only Rear Admiral and the entire Rebel navy!

Confederate railroad engines were abandoned as Semmes and his sailors commandeered one and fired it up.

"Where are the other trains? I've got to get my men out of here!"

"The *other* trains?" snorted the brakeman. "Y'all kiddin', Admiral? There ain't no trains left! And there ain't likely to be none 'til the damnyankees get here! Even if there were, they couldn't get past Burkeville Junction. Phil Sheridan and his cavalry is due there in a little while."

"To hell with Sheridan!" Semmes stormed. "Come on, men, we'll damn sure find *something* to get us out of here!" But a few of his men didn't share Semmes' optimism and despaired of reaching safety when they heard about Sheridan's drive to cut the R&D line to Danville. They were positive that the mighty Semmes, who had managed to slip through every trap set for him by the Yankees, had at last been beached for good. So they slipped into the mob and struck out for themselves.

Semmes and the remainder of his men plowed through the packed depot. In the yards stood a string of ramshackle wooden coaches. Vandals had pilfered everything that wasn't bolted down and Semmes wondered whether the cars would hold together even as far as Amelia Court House, more than 30 miles this side of Burkeville, if he managed to couple them all into a train — assuming he was enough of a magician to pull a locomotive out of the smoke-pungent haze over burning Richmond.

The cars were crammed with wild-eyed civilians who were kicking, clawing, and punching anybody who tried to follow them aboard. Dozens more were crawling along the roofs of the coaches and warding off stones thrown by those who would knock them off so they could grab their places. Like those inside, they seemed positive that providence would supply a locomotive, marshal the scattered cars into a train, and whisk them beyond the reaches of the hated Yankees before Sheridan cut the line a Burkeville Junction.

Semmes ordered his men to empty the cars.

"I'm going to put together a train for my troops," he told the civilians to quiet their protest, "and you'll be welcome to whatever room is left after I get my men aboard."

Far down the tracks, standing on a weed-covered siding, Semmes found a four-wheel switch engine which he guessed was easily as old as he was. There wasn't a wisp of smoke coming from her outlandish stovepipe of a stack and her rusty boiler was many weeks cold. It was anybody's guess whether she would be able to held together to Burkeville, much less all the way to Danville.

"Who's ever goin' to be able to fire up that thing?" asked a boatswain's mate.

Fortunately for the South, Semmes maneuvered at his optimistic best when the situation was at its blackest. "We are!" he beamed. "Have you forgotten, boy, that the days of the sailing navy are over? This is the age of steam. You marine engineers ought to be able to figure her out and have a fire going in a jiffy. She can't be too much different from our *Sumter* or *Alabama*."

"What ya gonna use for wood, Admiral? There's none in this here tender."

"That'll be your job. Go find some!"

Three railroad officials, gaunt men in high black hats and severe frock coats, hurried across the cinder-strewn yards toward Semmes.

"See here, what are you doing?" demanded the paunchiest official.

"I'm doing what you men should have done hours ago. I'm putting together a train to get my troops out of here, with as many civilians who hate the thought of living around

Yankees, seeing as how you've taken it upon yourselves to toss in the towel for the Confederacy."

"You're insane!" snapped the bearded one. "You'll never make it to Danville. Our telegrapher at Burkeville Junction just reported that General Sheridan's cavalry is getting closer and should be there about noon, the rate he's going. Some people say his advance parties are there already. Sheridan will tear up the rails and put you in the ditch before you can get through there."

"You don't even know if the track is clear," argued the other. "Here! Look at these." Semmes grabbed a sheaf of flimsy train orders. "Hold all Richmond trains!" said one dispatcher. "Come to Richmond with all engines and empty passenger cars and boxcars you can pick up" said another. "Richmond is being evacuated. Arrange for all track possible in Danville."

"See," said the official, "you're liable to hit another train coming this way head-on! And it might be loaded with explosives. It'd blow you and your Navy sky high.

"Then you don't mind if I try to make it?"

The three looked into the stern-faced Admiral's piercing blue eyes and saw his determination.

"Most assuredly we do! Where do you get off stealing our trains? You're not on the high seas now, Admiral! You're stealing private property that belongs to a Southern company! Just who the hell do you think you are?"

"I sir," said Semmes, making an overly polite, low, sweeping bow, "am Rear Admiral Raphael Semmes of the Confederate Navy and I hereby christen this train The *Alabama II*. My sailors will serve as her crew if your men won't. And when I'm finished with the locomotive and cars, you're welcome to take them back. Now if you'll excuse me, gentlemen, I'll see about setting sail for Danville."

Semmes dismissed the officials with a wave of his arm and strode off down the tracks.

"I'll bring charges of grand larceny," the paunchy one stormed after him. "I'll have you called up on the carpet before Jeff Davis! You can be a pirate on the high seas, but you'll not get away with stealing one of our trains!"

"Put your backs against these cars and push!" Semmes ordered his men, ignoring the outraged railroaders. "And, hurry! Shove those cars together over there and couple 'em."

Nudging the coaches together by hand proved no more difficult for Semmes' beefy seamen than running 'round the capstan while bringing up the *Alabama's* anchor. Semmes loaded his men aboard and posted guards with orders to shoot. He wasn't going to tolerate any more desertions. Then he hurried across the yard to the switch engine.

"How's that teakettle perking?" Semmes called out to his marine engineers.

"Fine, sir. We think we could build a good head of steam if only we could find some firewood."

"There!" said Semmes, pointing to a picket fence around a shack beyond the roundhouse. "What's wrong with that!"

"That's not firewood, Admiral. At least not the kind we need."

"It'll do until we get to a wood station," Semmes argued. "There must be a dozen of them between here and Danville."

The sailors hurriedly kicked the fence down, smashed the wood into small pieces and, in bucket brigade fashion, tossed the kindling into the tender. The naval engineers soon built a fire and steam hissed from the boiler. Semmes climbed up into the grimy cab. The engineer shoved the throttle forward and the locomotive inched ahead, creaking and cranking, its wheels squealing their protest against being awakened from their long sleep.

How Semmes figured out the maze of switches in the R&D yards will forever remain one of the war's mysteries. In 30 minutes he managed to push, pull, and coax the grunting locomotive into assembling all the cars into one train.

Semmes face was caked with soot as he tugged on the whistle cord. Two hoots brought a hundred civilians scurrying across the yards and aboard the already crowded train. Others clawed themselves up onto the roofs of the coaches.

"Cast off!" Semmes told the engineer, "I mean, let's highball!"

The engineer eased the throttle forward. The dinky engine coughed and gasped and a jet of smoke and cinders shot from the grotesque stack. Its bell clanged importantly and steam spewed from the cylinders as the drivers inched the wheels ahead. They spun when the slack ran out and the train threatened to stop, but continued to move slowly forward. A cheer went up from inside the coaches as the *Alabama II* started down the ways of the Richmond & Danville yards and crept west along the James River bank. The train was barely out of the yards when the engineer gasped.

"Admiral Semmes! Look!"

Semmes leaned out the cab window. Ahead loomed a slight hill.

"We'll never make it up that grade, Admiral, not with this old goat feeding on busted fence boards for fuel!"

The train slowed.

"Give her all you've got!" Semmes urged.

"I am, sir. I've got the throttle all the way forward now!"

The train clanked to a crawl, then stopped. Black smoke and cinders spewed from her stack and the wheels spun desperately as the engine strained.

"Try sand!"

The engineer tugged at the lever. Sand spurted onto the rails. Still the wheels refused to take hold. Sparks flew.

"Shake those grates!"

The fireman did as Semmes ordered, and the squat locomotive struggled, panted and screamed. No use.

Semmes looked across the James River at the enormous cloud of charcoal grey smoke hovering over Richmond and wreathing the city's seven hills. The skyline was etched with sheets of flame as block after block of homes was swallowed by the inferno. The Tredegar Iron Works, center of the Confederacy's munitions supply, was aflame and the hubbub from the city was punctured by shattering blasts from bursting shells and boxes of fixed ammunition. The flashes from the explosives streaked through the sky like lightning in a thundercloud.

Off to Semmes' right drifted the blazing hulks of his wooden gunboats and he solemnly watched the flaming finish of the Confederate Navy — ships he, himself, had put the torch to only hours before so Grant could not turn them upon the South. The spouting flames touched off the magazine of one gunboat and the shattering blast threw huge chunks of timbers and bits of iron high into the sky.

Semmes, himself, torched the James River Fleet of the Confederate Navy so that Grant could not turn them upon the South.

Semmes studied the center of Richmond through his telescope. Hordes of Union troops were winding through the streets like long blue serpents and converging upon Capitol Square. Flanking them were slender lines of cavalry. Behind, rumbled the horse-drawn Union artillery.

"I'm afraid we're done for, Admiral," said the engineer. "They'll catch us for sure!"

"Why don't we do the next best thing." suggested the fireman. "If we cut the train in two, I'm sure we can get up this hill. Better that some of us get away to continue the war, than none of us."

Semmes allowed as how the fireman had a good point and he would have a hard time justifying his failure to take such action if they all were captured. He looked over toward Richmond again. The artillery had now taken up positions and Semmes wondered why in thunder they weren't firing upon the train. The Yankee cannons were in point-blank range and even the most unskilled artilleryman could wipe out the *Alabama II* at that short distance. Surely they must have spotted them. Could it be that, in their victorious occupation of the Confederate capital, they were blinded to the obvious prize of a trainload of Johnny Rebs?

"Back up! Take up slack! Then give her full throttle!" Semmes ordered. The engineer pulled back the lever. The coaches bumped harshly into each other. Then the engineer eased the bar forward again. The train jerked, yanking the cars viciously, and stopped after picking up only three feet. Semmes helped the fireman-master's mate and the boatswain's mate-brakeman pitch more fence wood into the firebox. The crotchety locomotive strained, but the added steam did no good. *Alabama II* was aground before she got out of town, and the 172-mile run to Danville seemed like halfway 'round the world.

Semmes looked at his watch. It was going on nine o'clock. If he didn't do something fast, Sheridan would get to Burkeville before he so much as got out of Richmond.

A sense of desperation and hopelessness gripped everyone aboard the train. Semmes could almost feel the Yankee hangman's noose tightening around his neck. It wasn't that he had committed a single act of piracy, but rather his astonishing degree of success in twisting the Union nose out of joint.

It's been said that some Southerners didn't have the foggiest notion of what they were fighting for. Not Semmes. If ever there was a rebel with a cause, it was Semmes. He was always ready to expound the reasons for his hatred of the "money-hungry northern mercantile interests" and power hungry Federalists who forced, so he argued, the South to fight. Slavery was a secondary issue as far as he was concerned. Consequently, he wasn't one whit sorry to see so many American flag ships go to Davy Jones's Locker.

Semmes had traveled north as a Confederate representative and bought munitions for the South, although the manufacturers themselves knew the arms might be used against their own sons. Afterwards Semmes took a ship, a converted excursion steamer nobody wanted, and sailed it out of New Orleans, past the flustered *USS Brooklyn,* and promptly made prizes of 18 New England merchant ships, most of which he burned to the waterline.

Union cruisers chased Semmes across the Atlantic and, after securely bottling him at Gibraltar, assured alarmed shipowners that they had heard the last of "Old Beeswax," whose jaunty mustache was a symbol of Semmes' contempt for the Yankee Navy. But Semmes slipped away to London, then back-tracked down to the Azores where he took command of the sleek new *Alabama*, a steam and sailing barkentine.

During the next 22 months Semmes wiped out a fleet of New England whalers, blasted the *USS Hatteras* to the bottom of the Gulf of Mexico in a 13-minute battle, and racked up a whopping total of 87 captured ships, an $8,000,000 blow to Northern shipping, to say nothing of the loss of prestige suffered by the Union Navy. The North saved partial face when the *USS Kearsarge* finally caught up with Semmes off Cherbourg, France, and pounded the *Alabama* to the bottom. But the Yankees were denied their final pound of flesh when Semmes escaped to Southampton, and was smuggled back to the Confederacy where he took command of the James River fleet guarding Richmond.

Semmes was sitting down to dinner at 4 o'clock Sunday aboard his flagship, the ironclad *Virginia*, anchored in the James, when a messenger arrived from Navy Secretary Steve Mallory's office.

General George Pickett's lines had crumbled at Five Forks. Lee was pulling his army back from Petersburg and hurrying south and west toward Danville before Sheridan's cavalry of between 10,000 and 12,000 men cut off retreat. Richmond was to be abandoned and Semmes was to destroy his fleet. "You will then join General Lee in the field with all your forces," Mallory ordered.

In short, Semmes, the Confederacy's top seadog, was to become amphibious and turn his sailors into infantrymen.

"I'll do it, too, if ever I can get this confounded train the hell out of here," Semmes raged. The clamor from Richmond grew louder as the sun tried to dissolve the ugly haze over the city. The only thing in Semmes' favor was the fact that the bridges between Richmond and the Manchester section of the city across the James were down. The additional hour it would take the Yankees to bridge the river might give Semmes enough time to escape if he cut his train in half.

"I'll not do it," he finally said, pounding his fist in his hand. "I'll not leave a single one of my men behind!" Semmes leaped down from the cab and bounded across the cinders toward the R&D Repair Shops at the other side of the yards.

"Let's have one last look over here. Maybe we can piece together another engine."

In a gloomy corner of the barn-like building stood a locomotive — a much newer one than the engine Semmes had stolen — and designed for high-speed passenger service.

"Hey!" shouted the shop superintendent, running

toward Semmes, "You can't take that engine! We're saving her ..."

"For what!" Semmes interrupted, "Grant's victory train?"

"No, to get out of here ourselves ..."

"The Confederate Navy needs her a helluva lot worse than you ever will," Semmes shot back.

"What right have you ..."

"I've got a trainload of soldiers who say I've got all the right in the world!"

Semmes turned to his engineers. "Get some steam up in her and we'll hook her onto the train."

In a few minutes steam was pulsating through her highly polished green boiler banded with shiny copper. Semmes stepped back and admired her four high red-rimmed driving wheels and her small pilot truck. The engine's crowning glory was her huge diamond stack. Semmes climbed up into the red-and-blue trimmed cab and felt the cheery glow of the fire roaring in her box. This, more befitting the style to which a Rear Admiral is accustomed, seemed as comfortable as the *Alabama's* gleaming quarter-deck.

The locomotive was backed down the track, its huge brass bell clanging impatiently, and softly kissed the coupling of the old switch engine. The links joined and the pin dropped into place.

"OK!" shouted Semmes. "Let's get rolling!"

The two engines tugged and the train slowly gathered speed as the Mutt and Jeff locomotives teamed to pull the *Alabama II* out of the Richmond yards. Fearfully, Semmes looked at his watch. Ten o'clock. He had two hours to get past Burkeville ahead of Sheridan, unless the Yankee cavalry had arrived ahead of schedule.

"With two engine doubleheading us out of here we ought to make it to Burkeville in half the time!" Semmes shouted over the pounding exhaust of the locomotive as it tried to smother the screeching protests of the switch engine clanking bravely behind. The train chugged west along the James for several miles, then followed the rails and bent southwesterly toward Burkeville, midway to Danville.

"Can't you push her any more?" Semmes shouted.

"No, sir," said the engineer. "not without pulling a bar, and especially not with this fence wood for fuel."

"There's a fueling station up ahead!" the fireman called out. The engineer put on the brakes and the coaches lurched forward as the train slowed, nearly pitching Semmes against the firebox door. Clearly, the naval engineer at the throttle had a lot to learn before he mastered smooth stops. Semmes himself, was beside his men as they swarmed over the wood pile and heaved chunks of firewood until both tenders were filled.

Five minutes later the train was zipping through the Virginia countryside, jet black smoke spewing from the two locomotives and showering the rattling cars behind with sparks and cinders. Telegraph poles flicked past like fence pickets. It was after 11 o'clock and the sun was standing high in the sky, but they hadn't even reached Amelia Court House of Jetersville, and between there and Burkeville lay a long stretch of track.

Semmes yanked the whistle cord as the train swished past way stations. Baffled farmers looked at the grotesque train pulled by the fancy high-stepper and the nondescript bucket of bolts.

"Any more speed in this teakettle?" Semmes called out.

"I don't dare try, sir," shouted the engineer, without pulling his head in the cab window. "I'm pushing her over the limit now. If Sheridan's advance patrols got here first and loosened the rails I'd never stop her. We'd fly a hundred yards before we hit the ditch."

Semmes looked anxiously from the cab for some sign of guerrillas or Yankee cavalry up ahead. He saw a flimsy trestle rushing toward him. Suppose it had been dynamited and set to blow when the *Alabama II* chugged onto the middle of it? The train clattered over the bridge and the hollow clickety-clack of the spinning wheels echoed in the cab as Semmes braced himself for a splitting BOOM and a sickening plunge.

But nothing happened.

The *Alabama II* stopped briefly at Amelia Court House, an hour's run from Burkeville, where General Lee had waited for supplies that never came. There was no sign of the bustling activity of a few days earlier, but plenty of Rebel stragglers. Semmes hated to waste time, but he refused to leave any fighting man behind if there was the faintest chance of putting him back in the field again.

In five minutes the train was puffing out of the cluster of buildings after picking up as many Confederate officers and soldiers as it could. Semmes looked back over the swaying cars and wondered how in the name of Jefferson Davis the refugees managed to stay on top of the jiggling coach roofs.

The train paused at Jetersville, half an hour from Burkeville, for more firewood and water. Semmes saw two black-frocked railroad officials hurrying toward the front end of the train.

"Looks like word of our cruise has preceded us," said Semmes. "Must be the wires aren't down yet."

The lankier of the two greeted Semmes with a toothy grin.

"We'll be much obliged if you'll give us back our train. We can take you the rest of the way to Danville. You've still got a husky ways to go, you know."

"We seem to be doing right well for ourselves," Semmes replied. "It couldn't be that you hope to save your skins from Sheridan, could it? If so, you're welcome aboard, but I'll do the navigating."

"That's absurd. You don't know the first thing about railroading. You're a Navy ..."

"I seem to have managed quite well up to now, no thanks to you people."

"You're a robber!" snapped the other with the beady eyes. "You're stealing our locomotives, our cars, and helping yourselves to our wood and our track, everything." He started up into the cab.

Semmes stepped forward, his eyes blazing and his mustache twitching.

"This is my ship! And I'll thank you to get the hell off my quarterdeck before I throw you off!"

The startled railroader backed down the steps and stood aghast on the ballast as Semmes swept his arm upwards and the train rumbled out of Jetersville. Semmes looked back over the saffron-colored coaches and wondered how a dozen more passengers had managed to get up onto the sloping roofs, and whether the tops of the cracker-box cars would support their added weight. Even the open vestibules were crowded.

Alabama II hurtled down the tracks as it streaked through the open Virginia countryside. Burkeville Junction was only a few miles ahead and Semmes leaned out from the window of the cab to sweep the area ahead with his telescope for some outline of the rail center's buildings. All he saw was the sun shining brightly upon the fields, green with early grass and spring flowers.

Farmers paused at their plowing of corn and tobacco fields to gape at the weird train with the overflowing load of passengers streaking past them. Even the R&D Dixie Flyer didn't zip as fast as this one did.

"Burkeville Junction ahead," called out the fireman as the sign board flashed past. Semmes swept the countryside with his telescope and then put it down because he didn't need it. A distant cloud of dust, plainly visible to the naked eye, was bearing toward them.

"Sheridan's cavalry!" gasped Semmes. "Give her all you've got!"

"I am, sir," said the engineer, not daring to take his eyes off the winding track ahead. Semmes refused to look, for fear he might see another train coming 'round the bend toward them, a fear which had haunted him all day.

Burkeville Junction's shacks and shanties and bridges and culverts and switches and crossovers flashed past as the *Alabama II* rocked and clattered through the town. A dumbfounded telegrapher looked up at the odd double-header train with the crazy Admiral hanging half way out of the lead locomotive cab, gun in hand.

"We're running low on wood again, Admiral."

"Can't stop!" Semmes told the fireman, "Sheridan's nipping at our heels."

In a few minutes Burkeville and the Yankee cavalry were a speck far behind the *Alabama II.*

Throughout the day the train hammered along the R&D's main line, pausing only twice to take on water while the seamen tossed as many chunks of firewood as they could into the tenders. The instant the tanks were filled the train highballed off again into the dusk.

Semmes was hardly aware of nightfall as the train hooted through towns and villages and in a little while its boxlike headlight bored into the darkness. The brilliance made the rails glisten. Semmes peered out into the night, hopping the headlight would not silhouette a barricade of broken rails, ties, or tree stumps piled by guerrillas.

"There she be, Admiral!" said the engineer, settling back in his seat.

Semmes looked from the cab window. A few miles ahead twinkled the lights of Danville. The *Alabama II* puffed into the city, its whistle shrieking victoriously and its bell clanging in celebration. Semmes, first off the train, hurried to the temporary headquarters of the Confederate Government. He reported his arrival to Navy Secretary Mallory, but word of the great train robbery of the Civil War had preceded him. President Davis was already fending off angry protests from the R&D's president.

Davis shrugged off the railroad's complaints while Semmes saw to it that his men pitched their hammocks aboard the *Alabama II,* because there was no barracks for them at Danville. Jeff Davis cited Semmes' daring by promoting him to Brigadier General and placing him in charge of artillery guarding the city, a singularly empty honor as it turned out.

History well records what a hell-for-leather sea raider Semmes was, but we can only speculate what he might have done in command of a rebel army. Rear Admiral and Brigadier General Raphael Semmes was in a muddy trench when word reached him, four days later, that Lee had met a cigar-smoking Yankee named Grant at a place called Appomattox Court House. The war was over.

Index

INDEX

108

INDEX

About the Author

PAUL DITZEL

Paul Ditzel, a historian and avid Civil War buff, has 18 books and over 600 articles for magazines to his credit, including those published in the *Readers Digest*. His best-selling book, *Fire Engines, Firefighters*, was submitted for a Pulitzer Prize in American History.

He holds a Master of Science Degree from Northwestern University, where he graduated with highest scholastic honors.

His well-researched and superbly written books and articles have won numerous awards.